Real World
Colouring Book
For Advanced Users & Adults

50 Images

Created From Real Life Photos For You To Colour As You Please.

ISBN 978-0-359-82367-3
90000
9 780359 823673

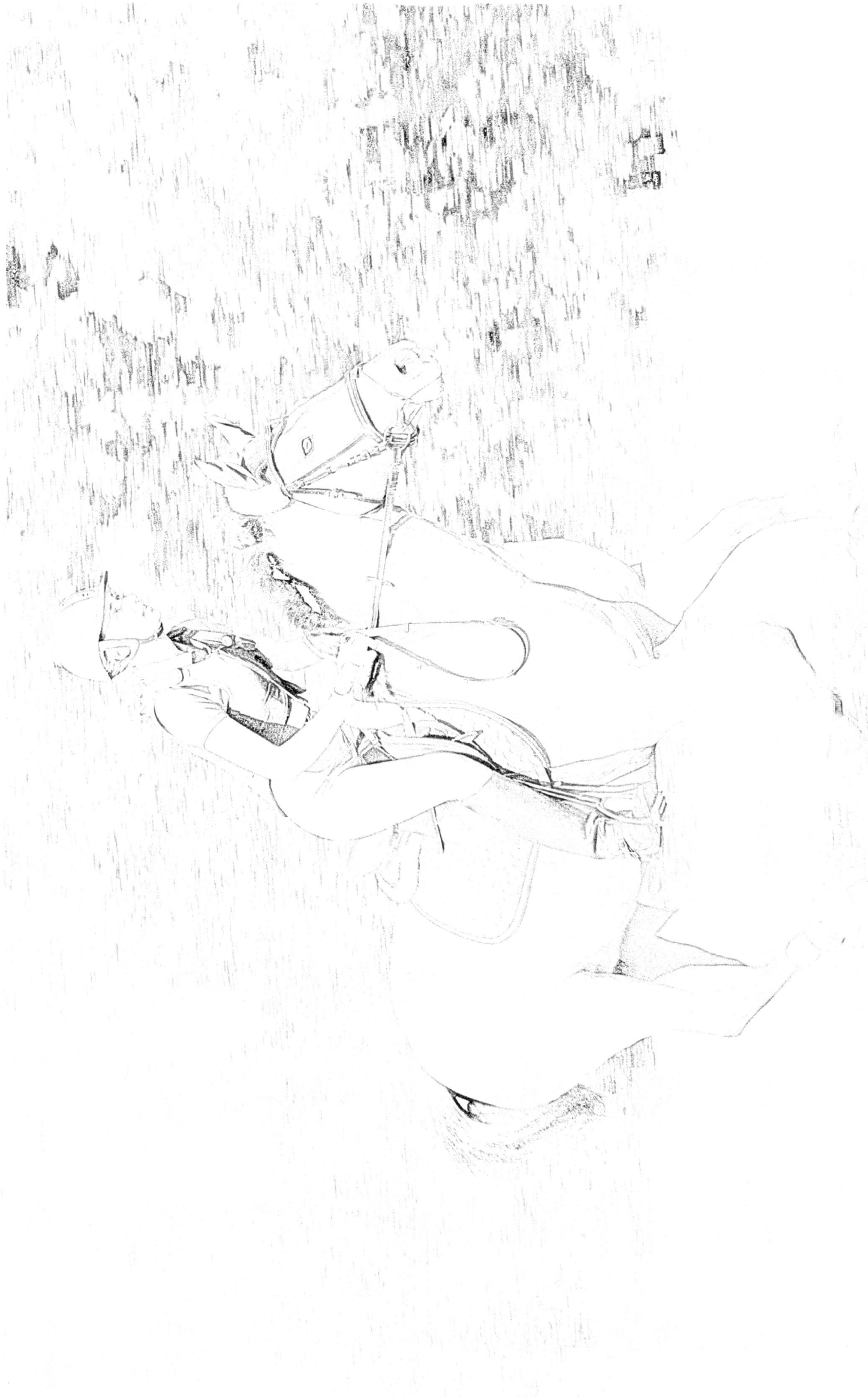

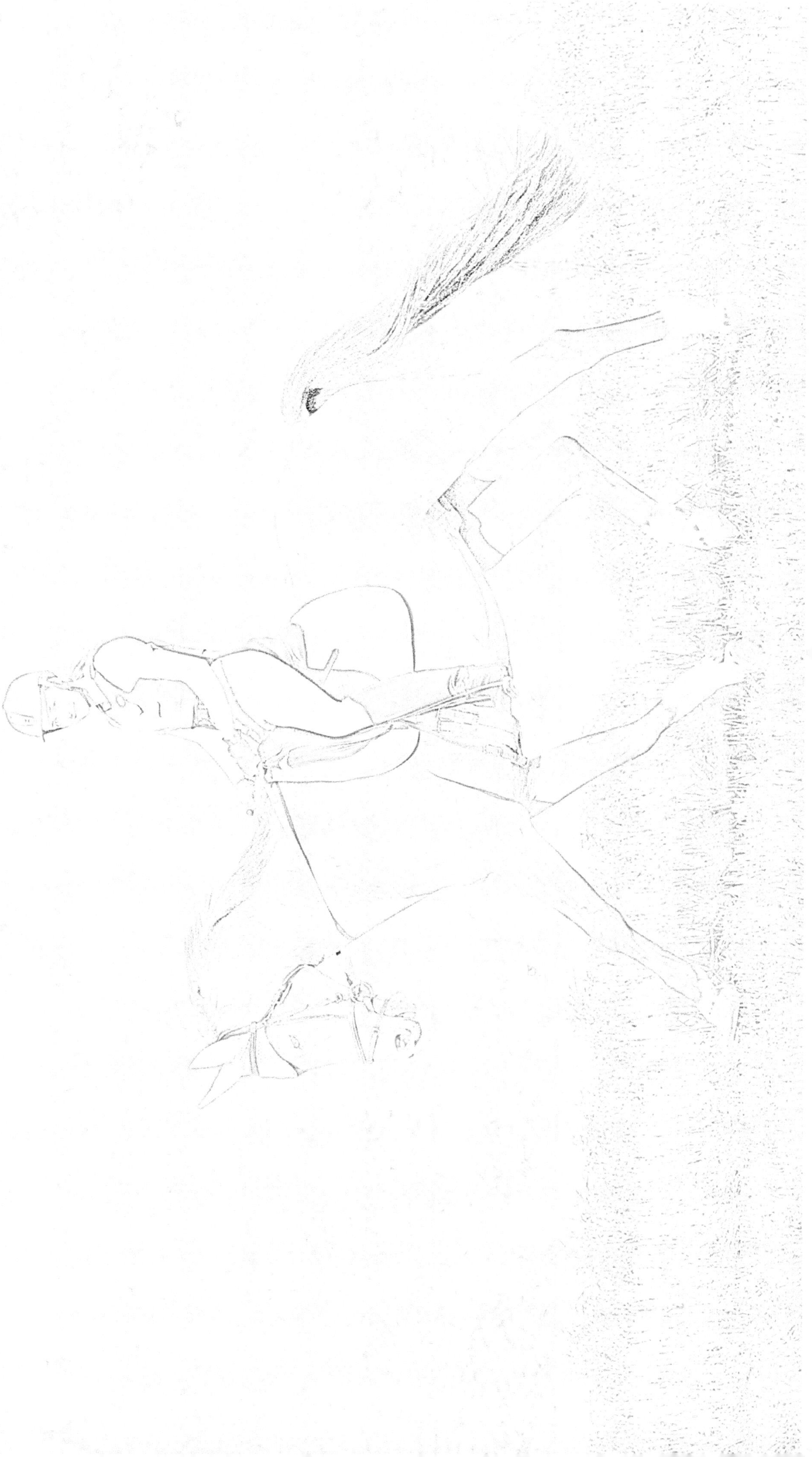

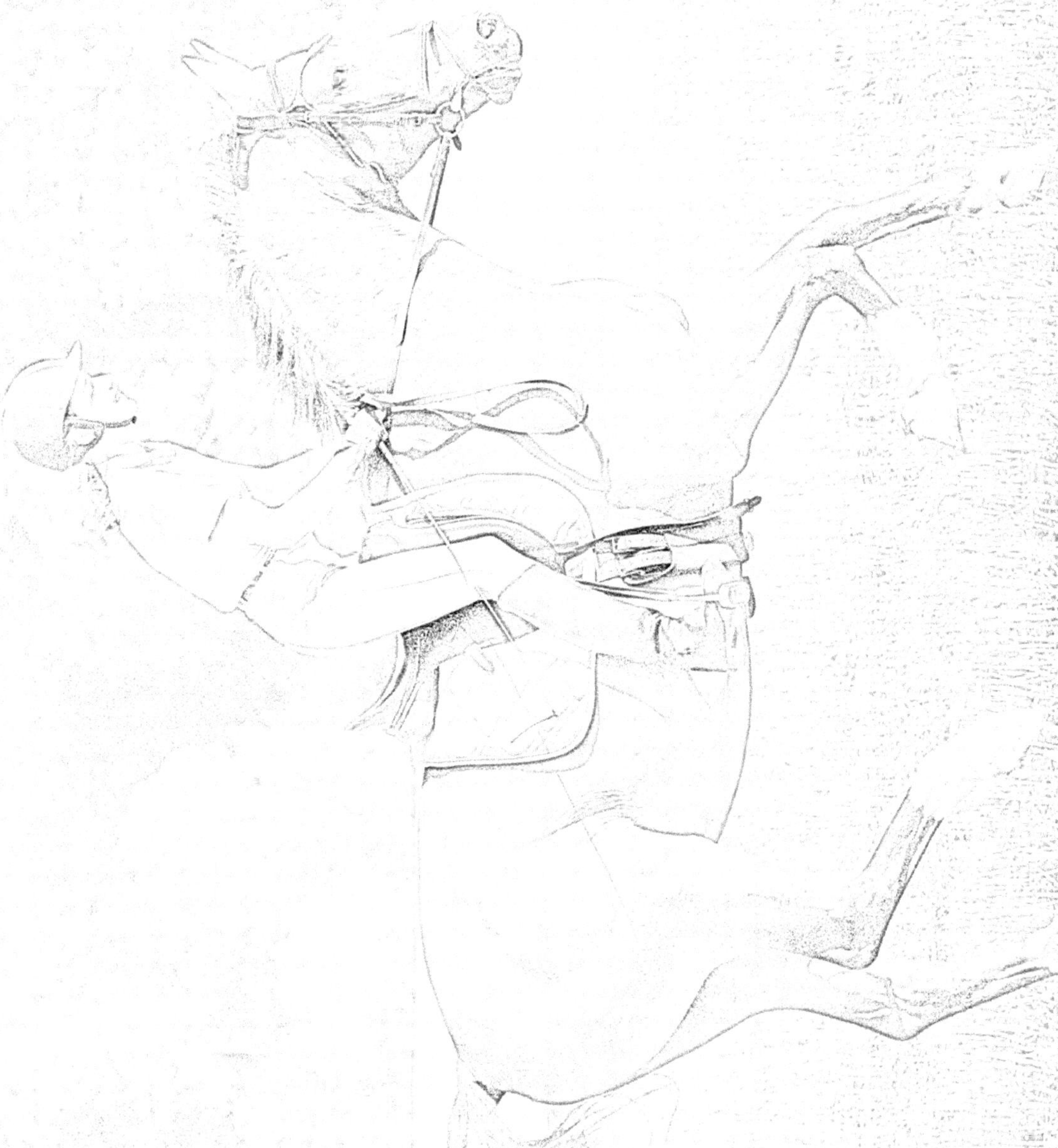

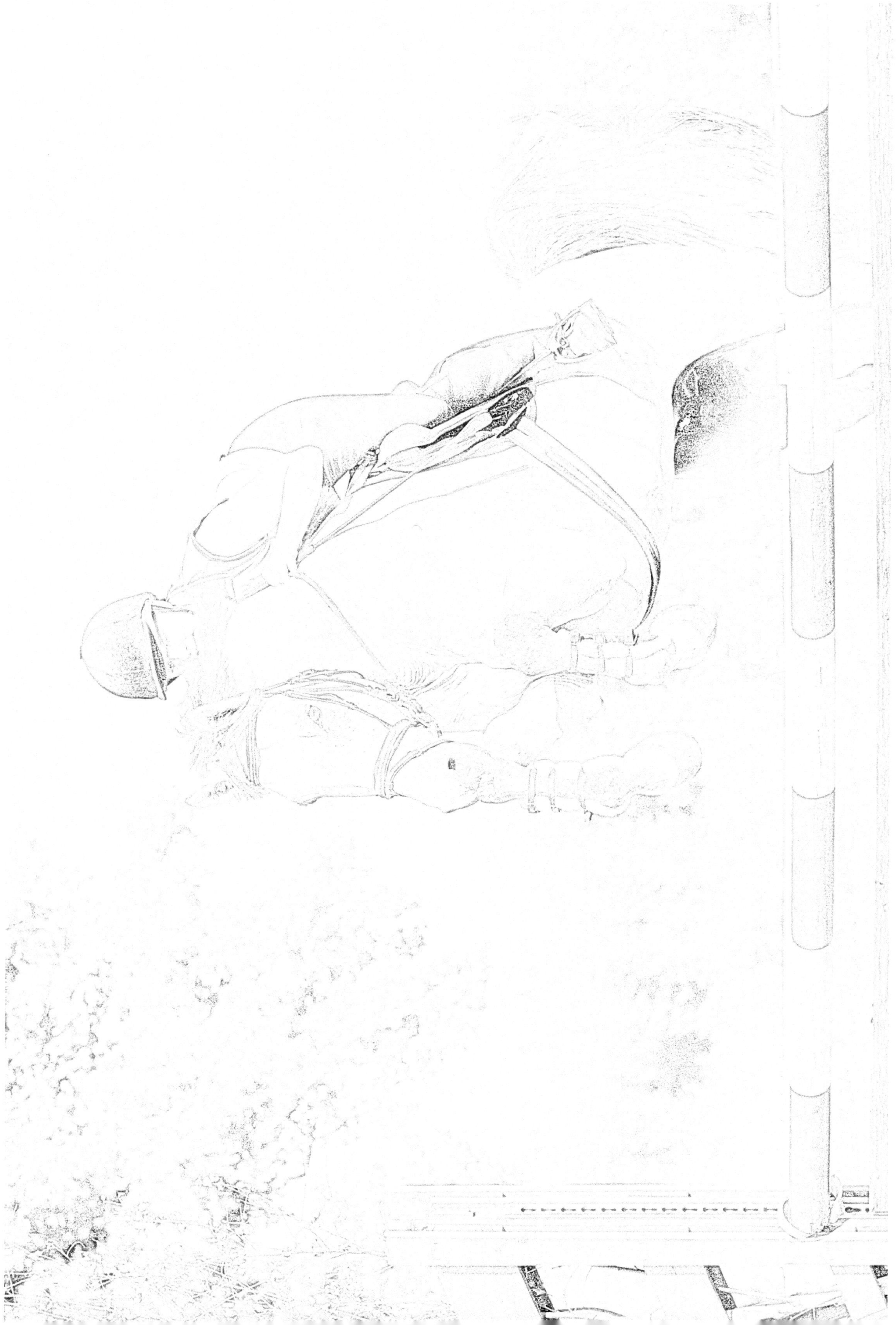

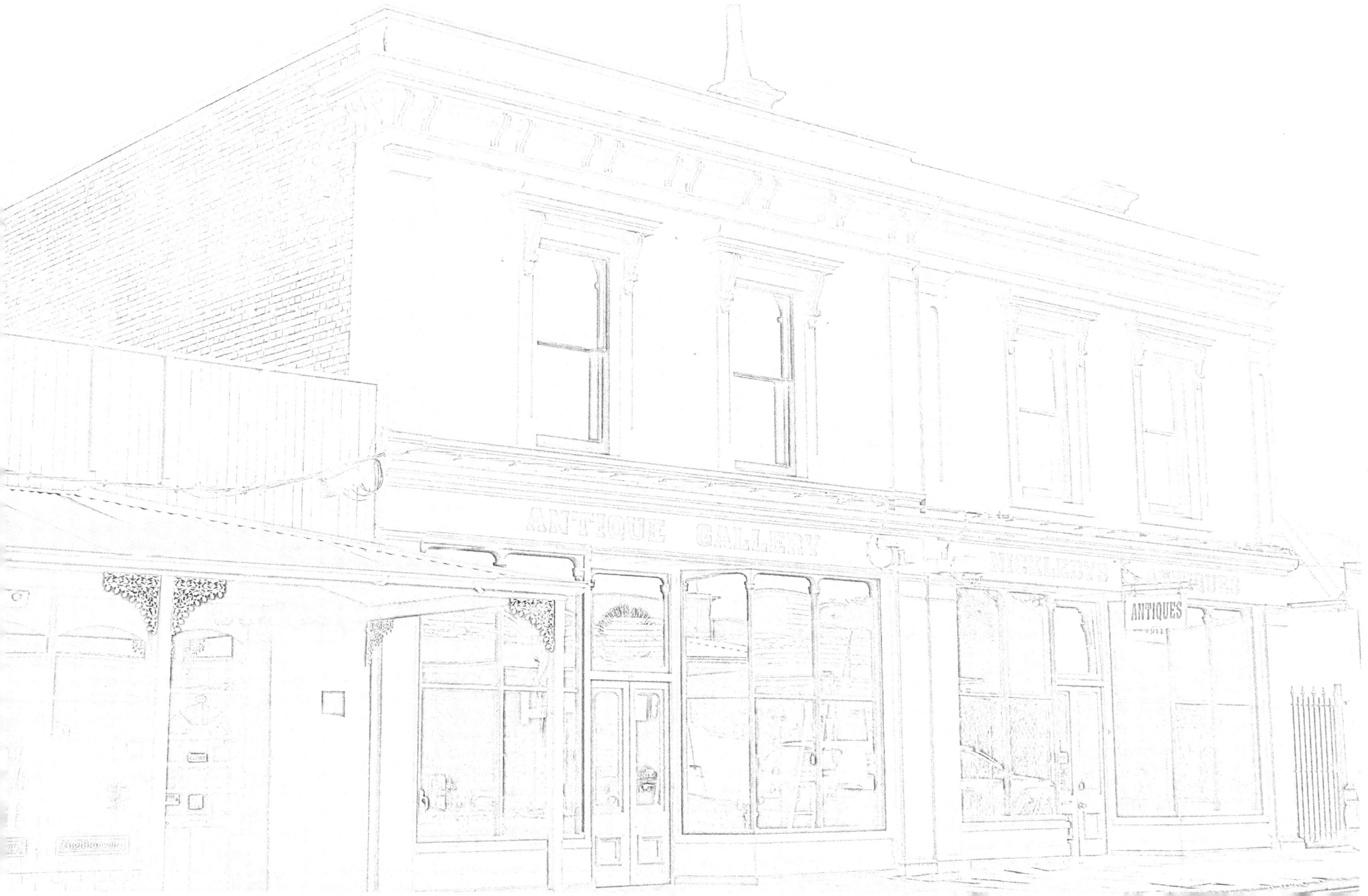
ANTIQUE GALLERY
NICKLEBYS
ANTIQUES

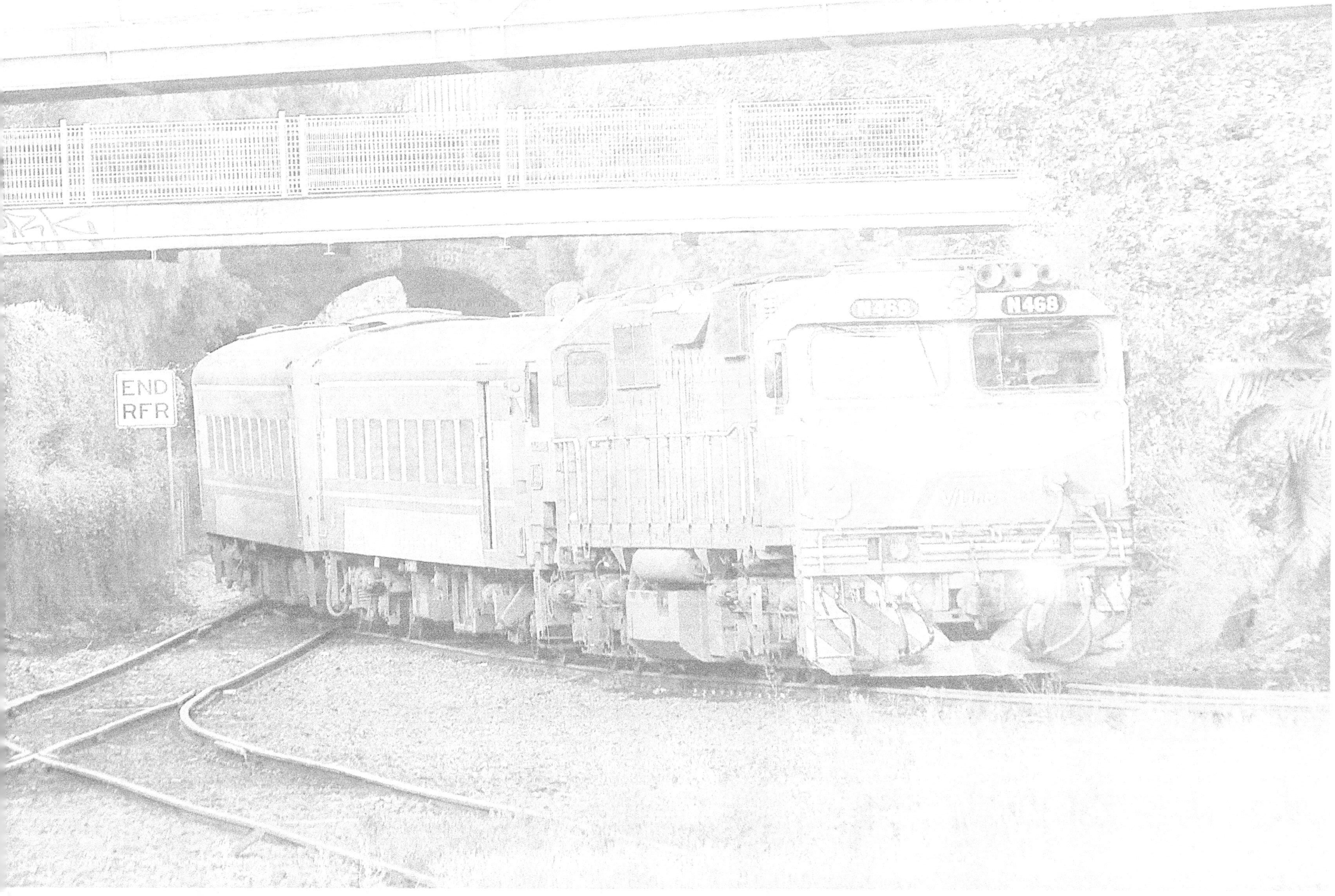
END
RFR
N468

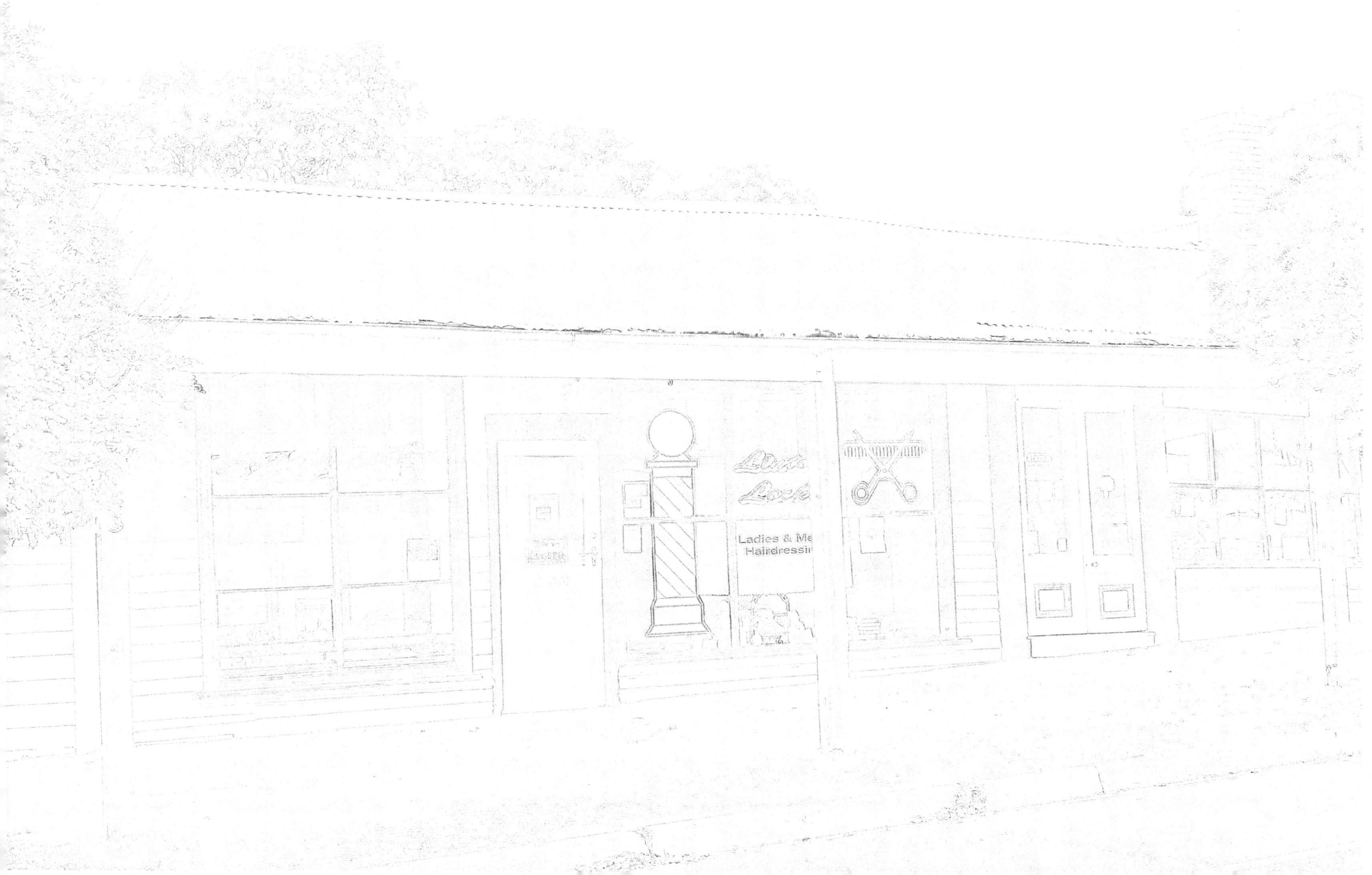
Ladies & Me
Hairdressi

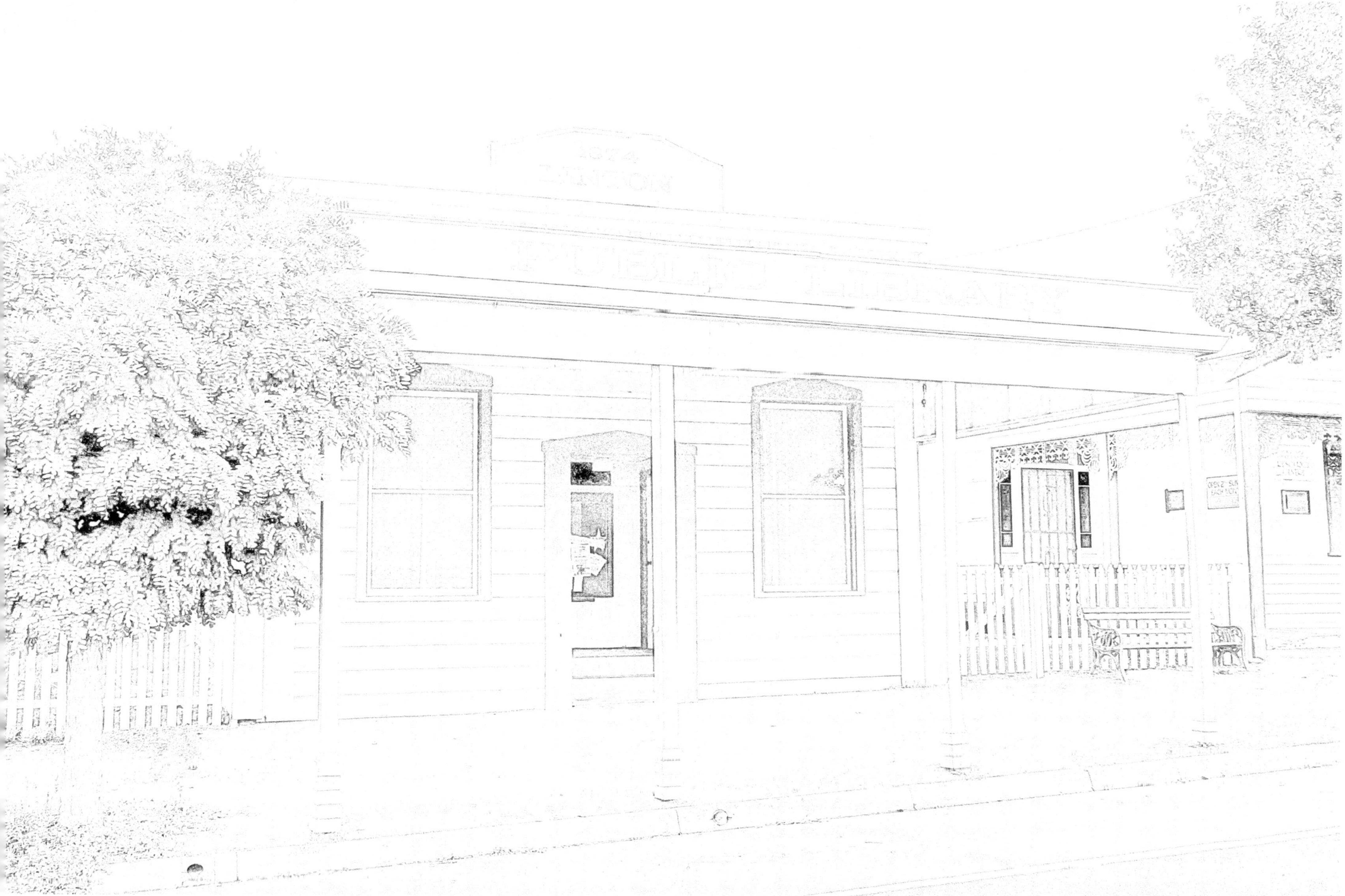
PUBLIC LIBRARY

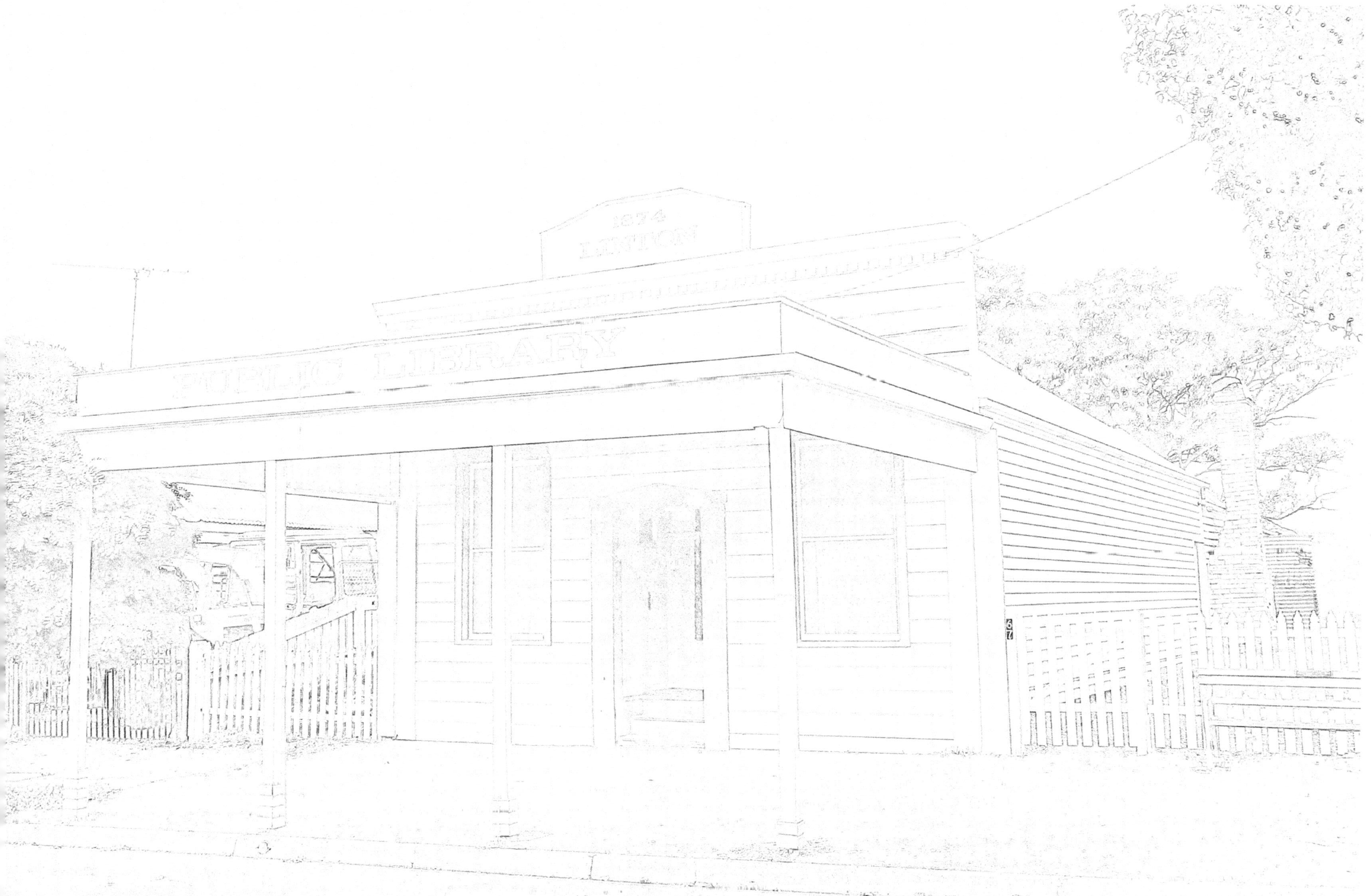
1874
LINTON
PUBLIC LIBRARY
67

NELSON BROS
PHONE 9
UNDERTAKERS
71

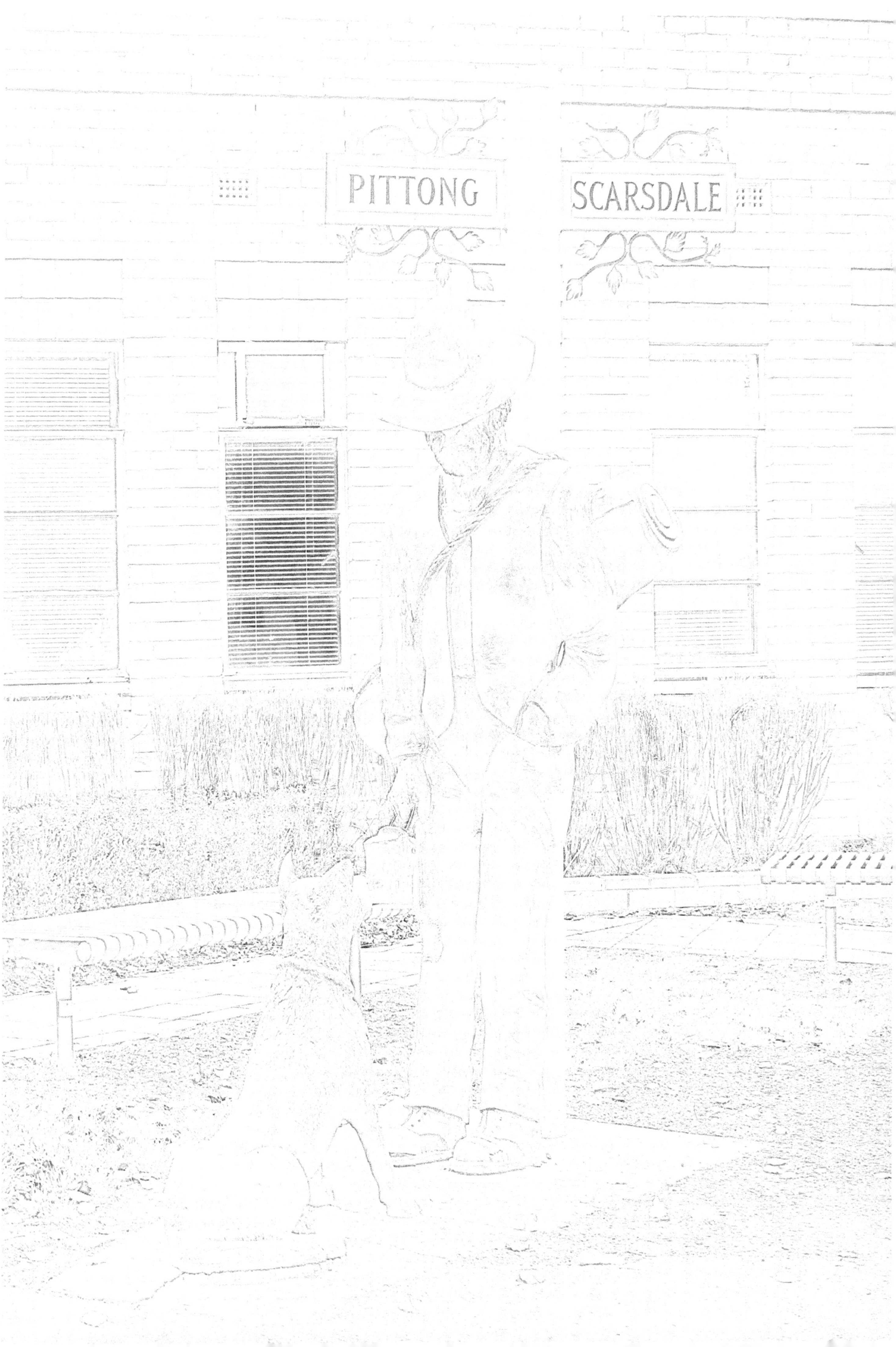
PITTONG
SCARSDALE

Giftware
Antique
CFA

RAILWAY HOTEL
BISTRO & BAR MEALS
ICY COLD BEER
BOTTLE SHOP
ESPRESSO
LATTES
All Day
LOUNGE

RECYCLED clothing

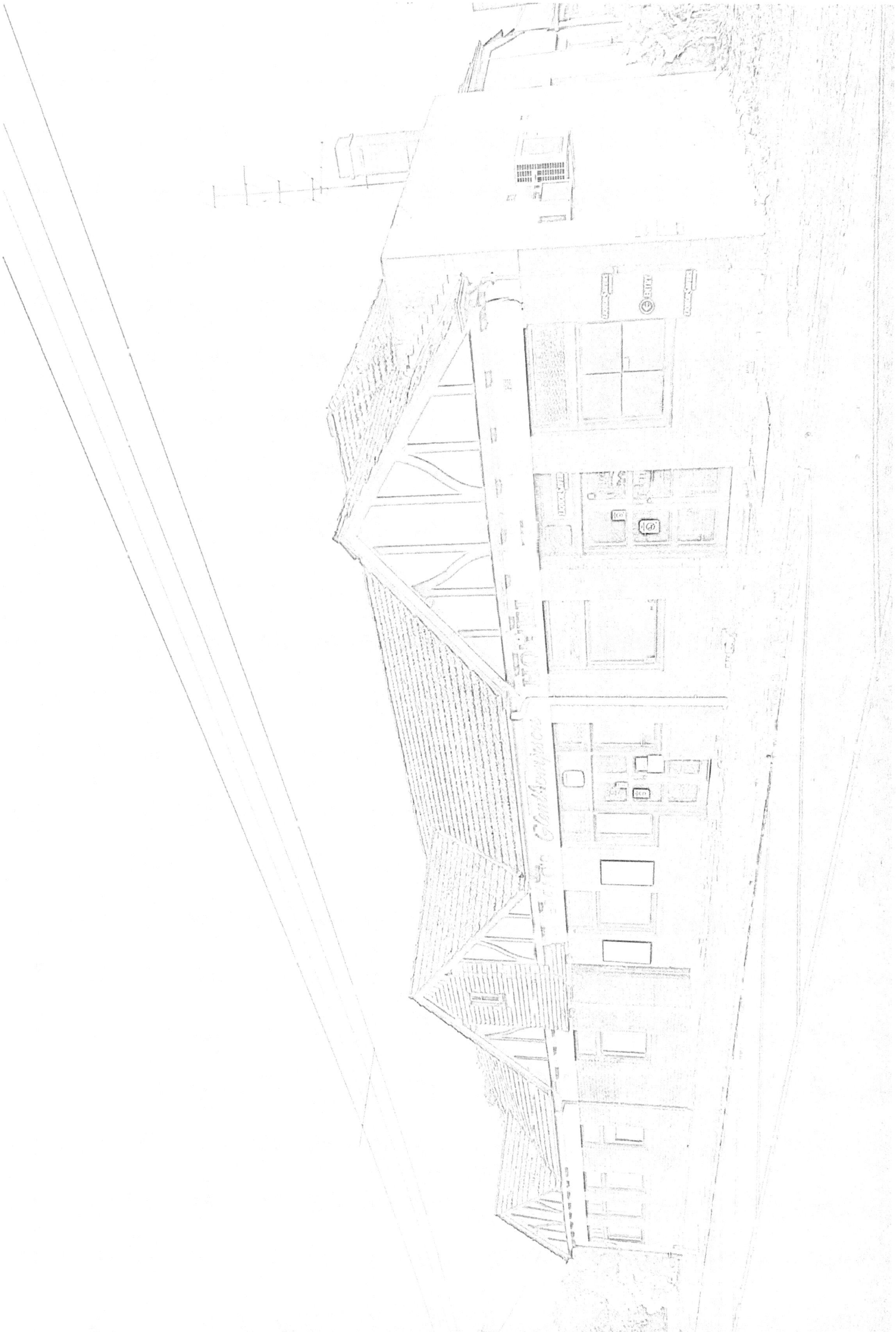

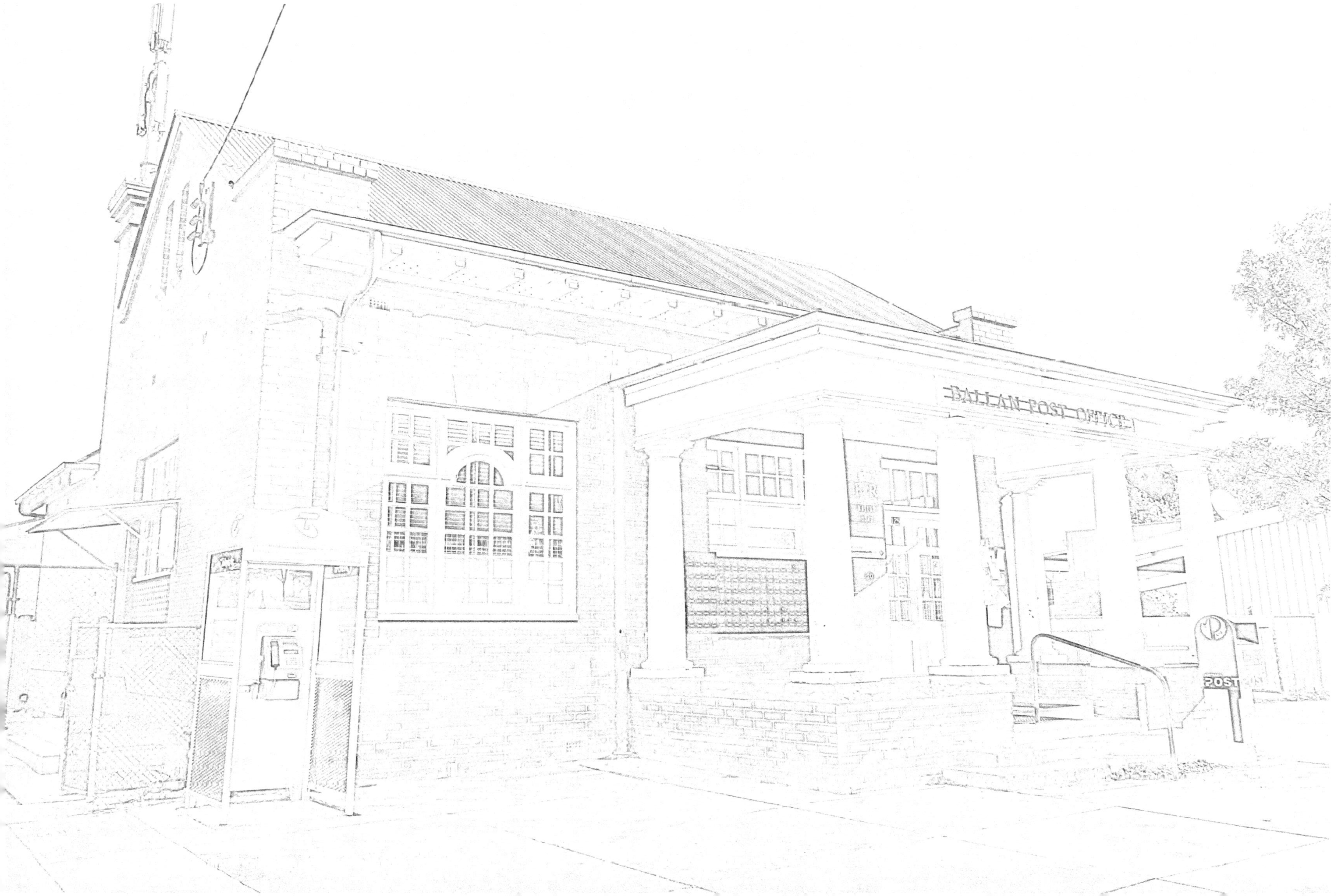
BALLAN POST OFFICE
POST

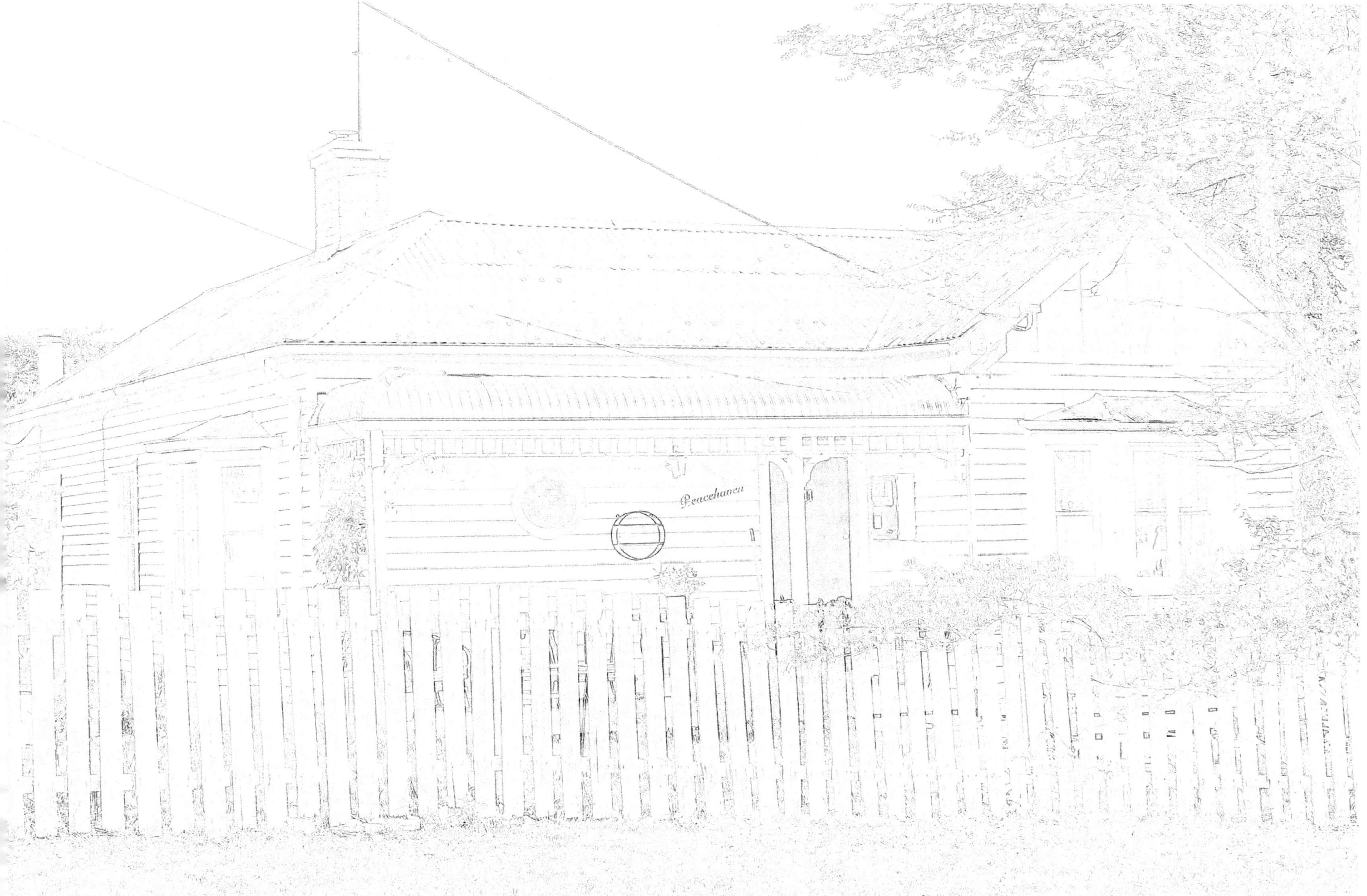
Peacehaven

LYONVILLE

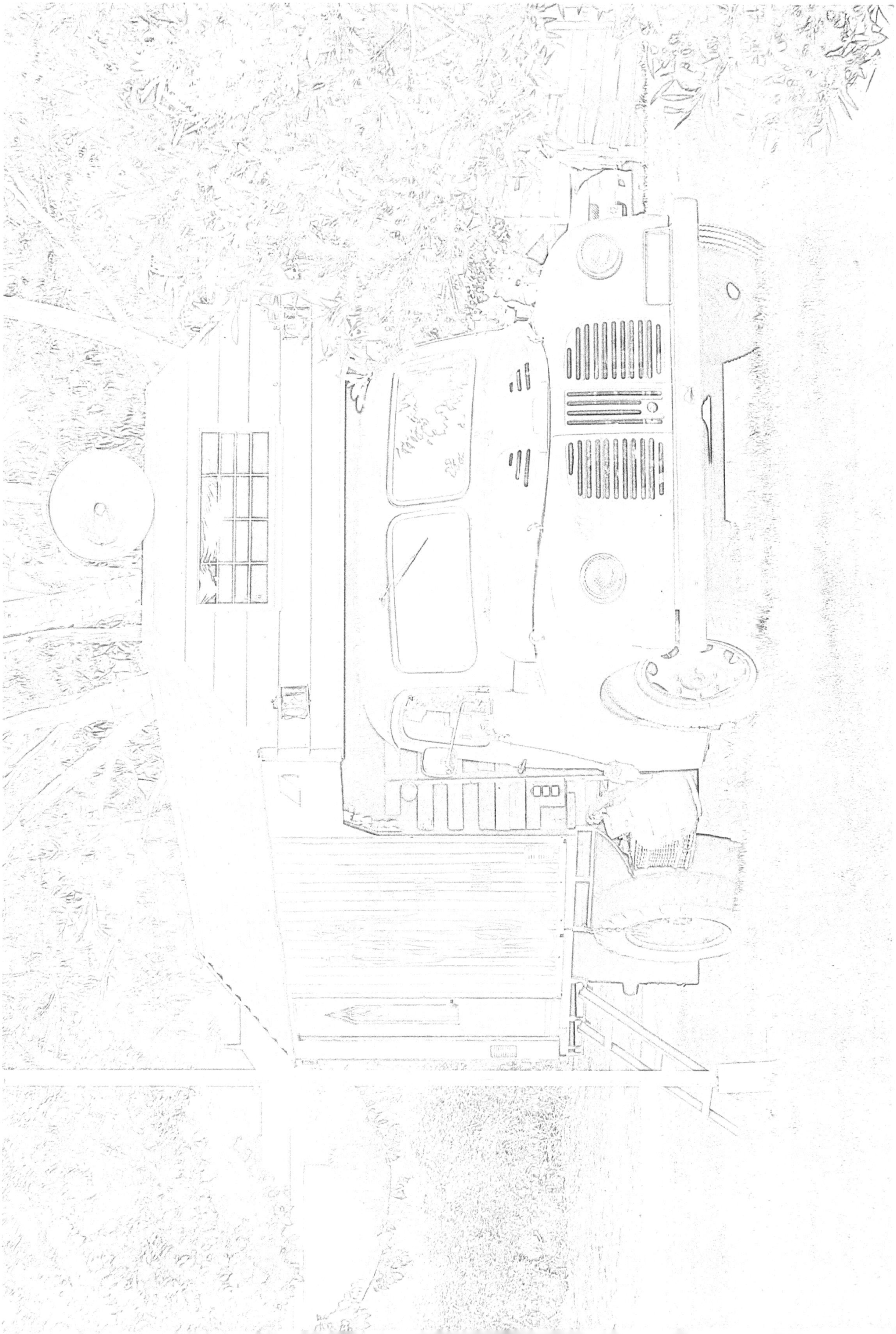

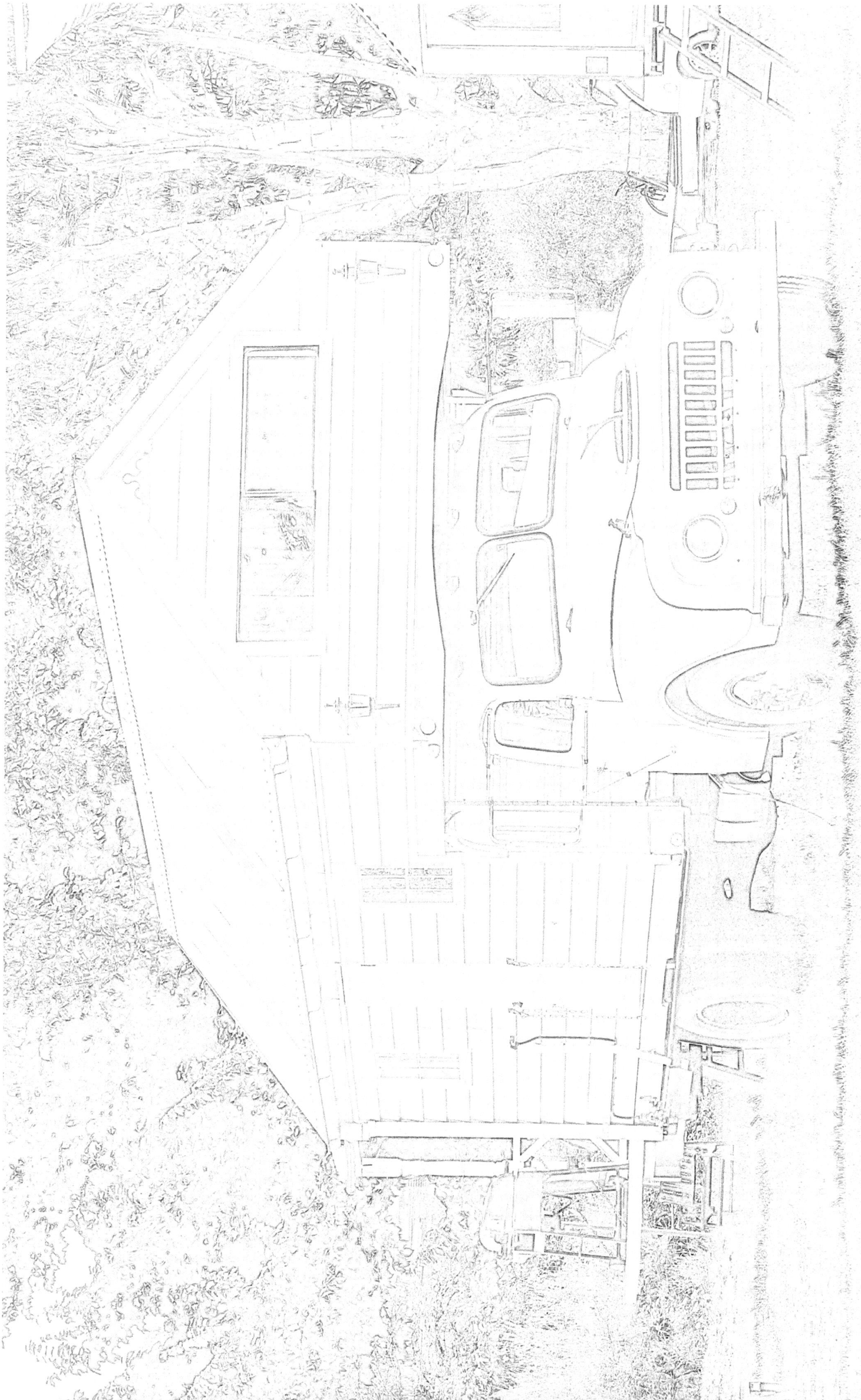

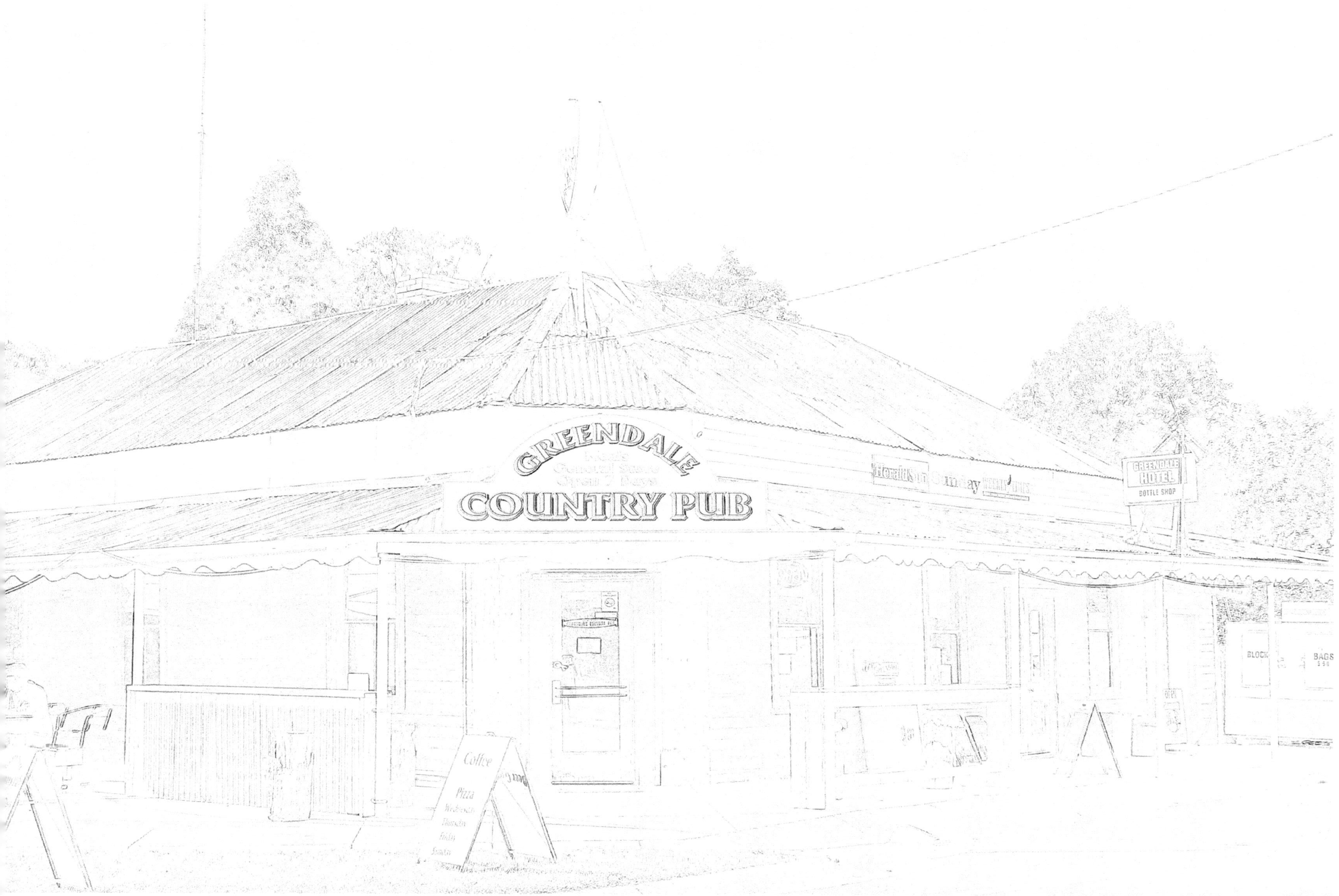
GREENDALE
COUNTRY PUB
GREENDALE HOTEL
BOTTLE SHOP
Sunday
Coffee
Pizza
BLOCK
BAGS

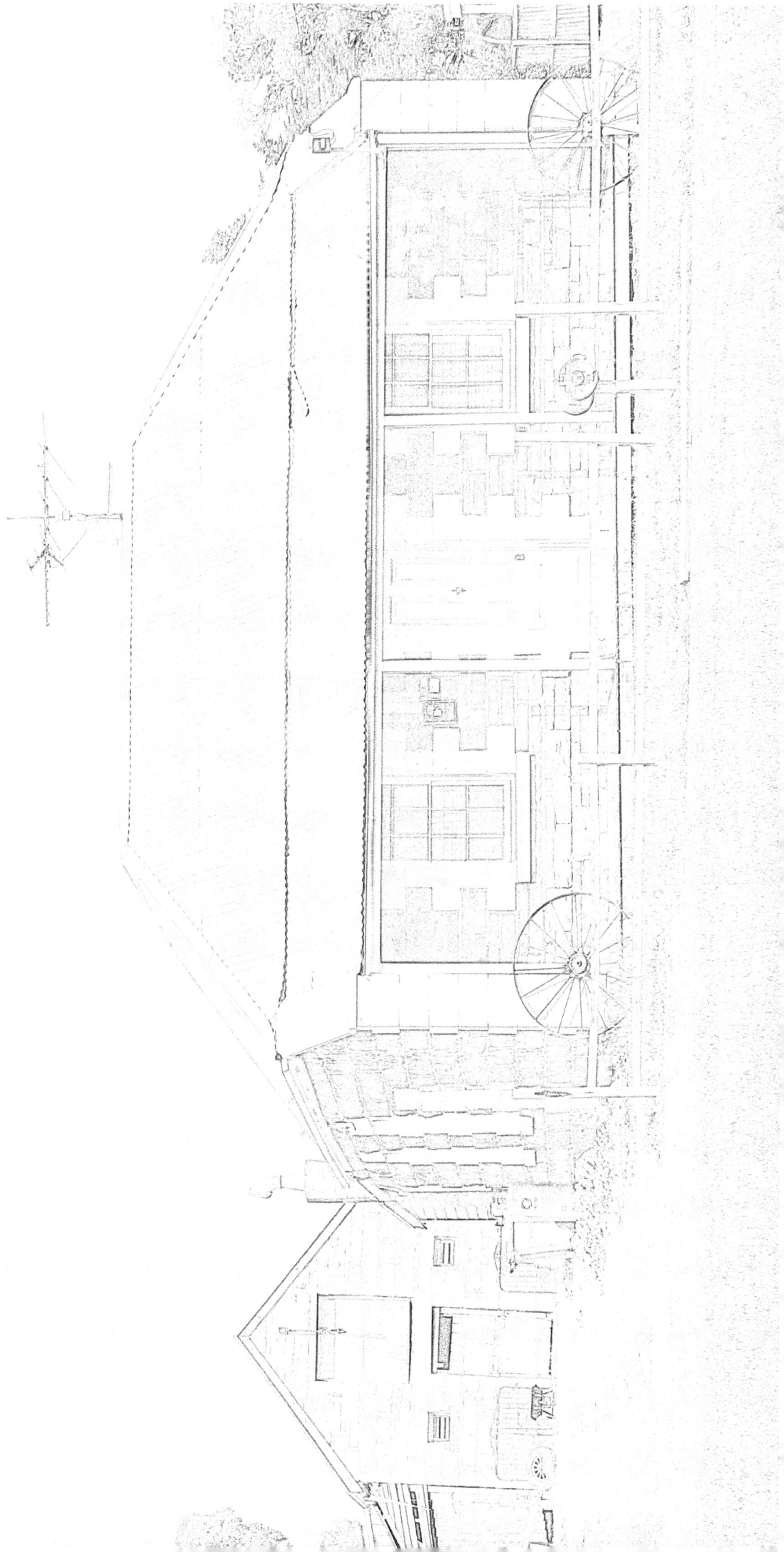

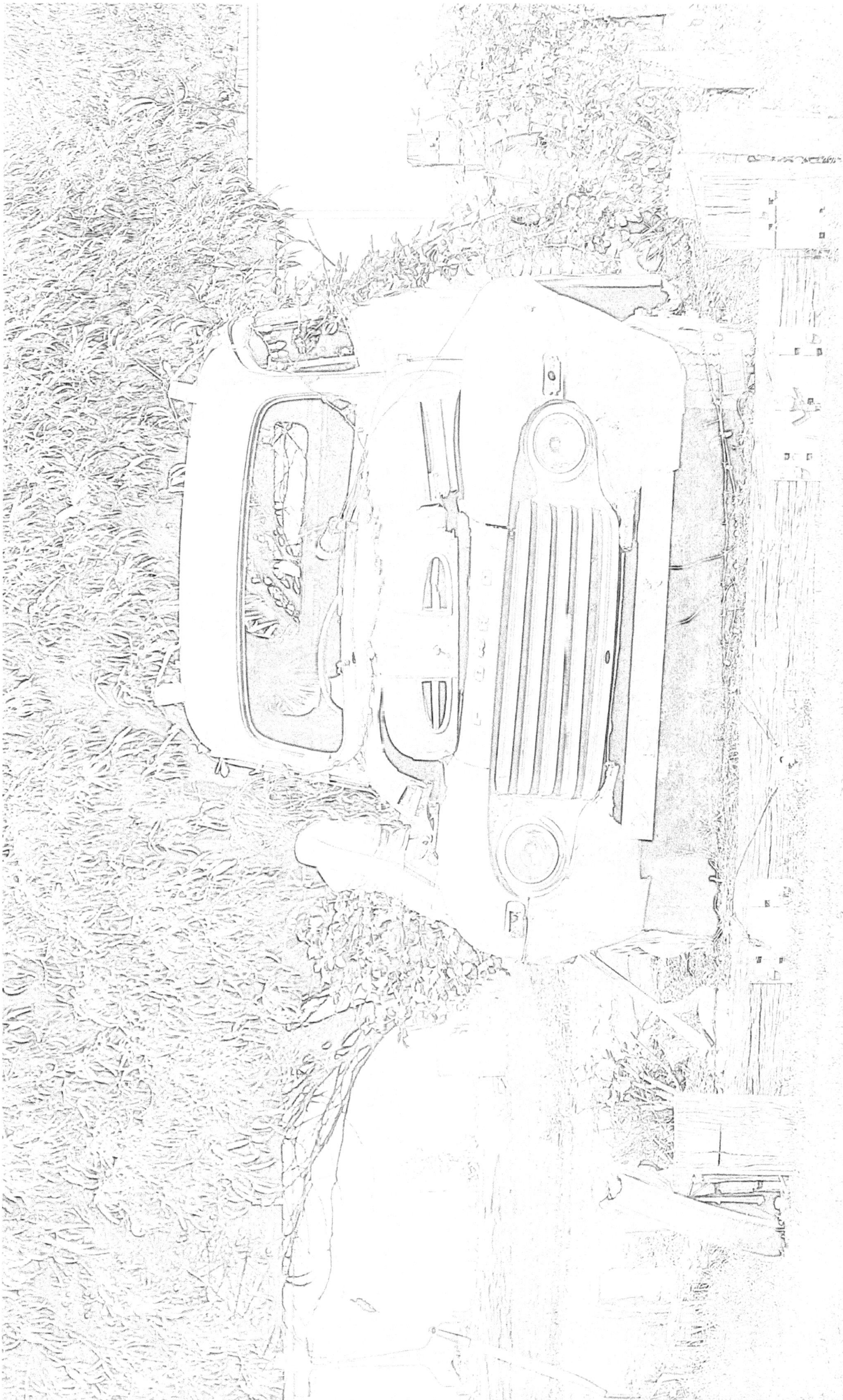

FREE LIBRARY
1877

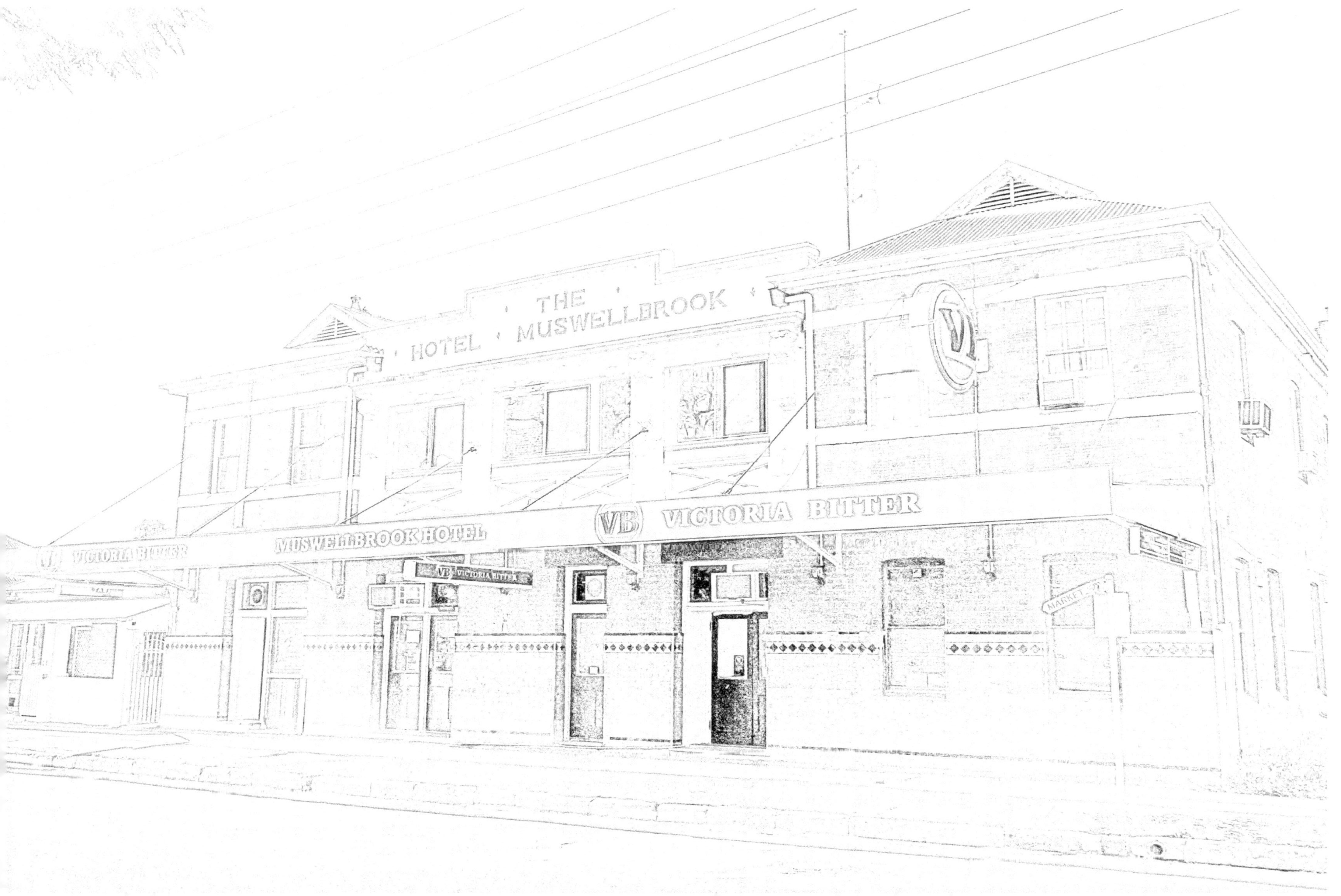
THE MUSWELLBROOK HOTEL
VB VICTORIA BITTER
MUSWELLBROOK HOTEL
VICTORIA BITTER
VB VICTORIA BITTER

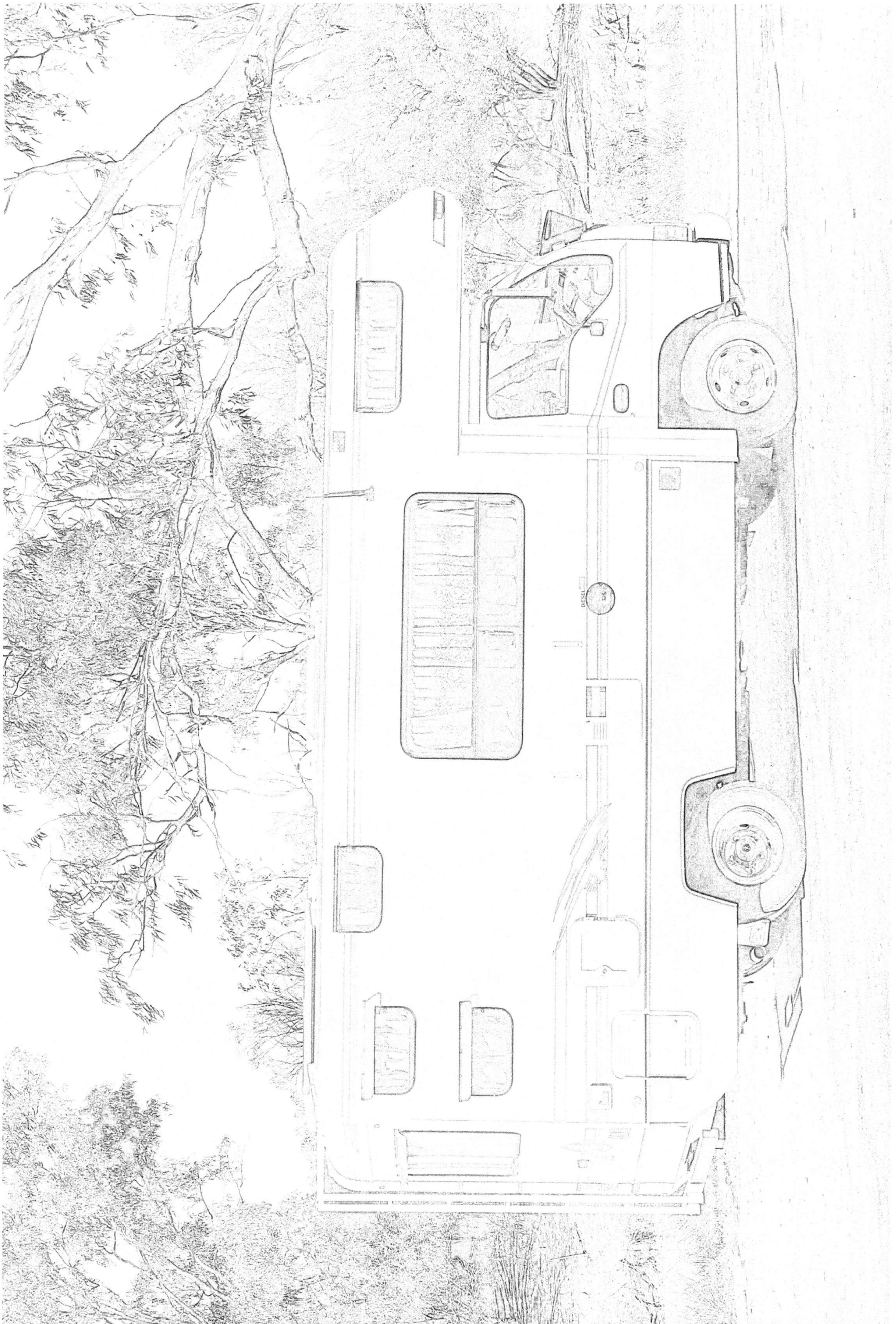
DIESEL

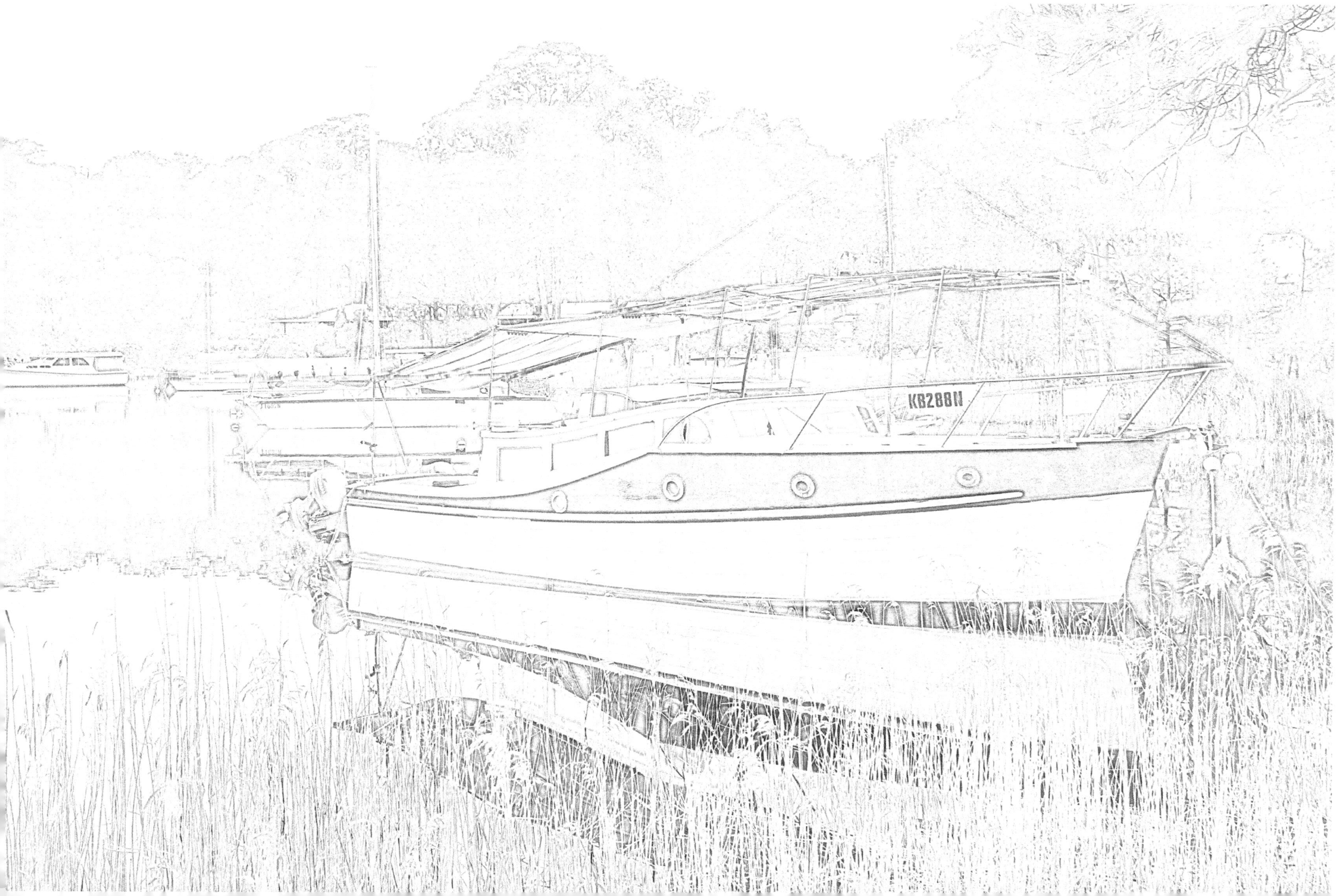
KB288N

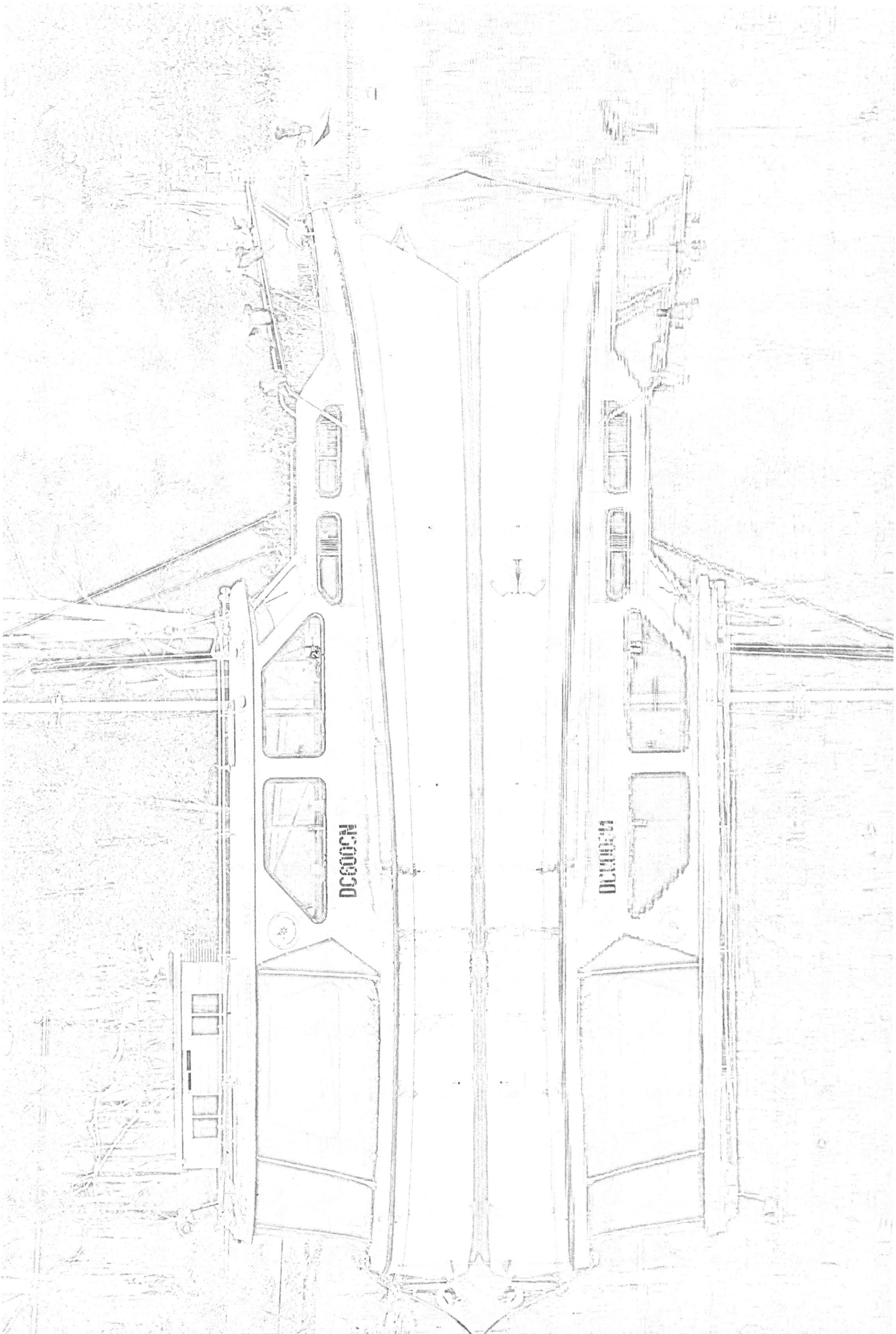
DC600CN

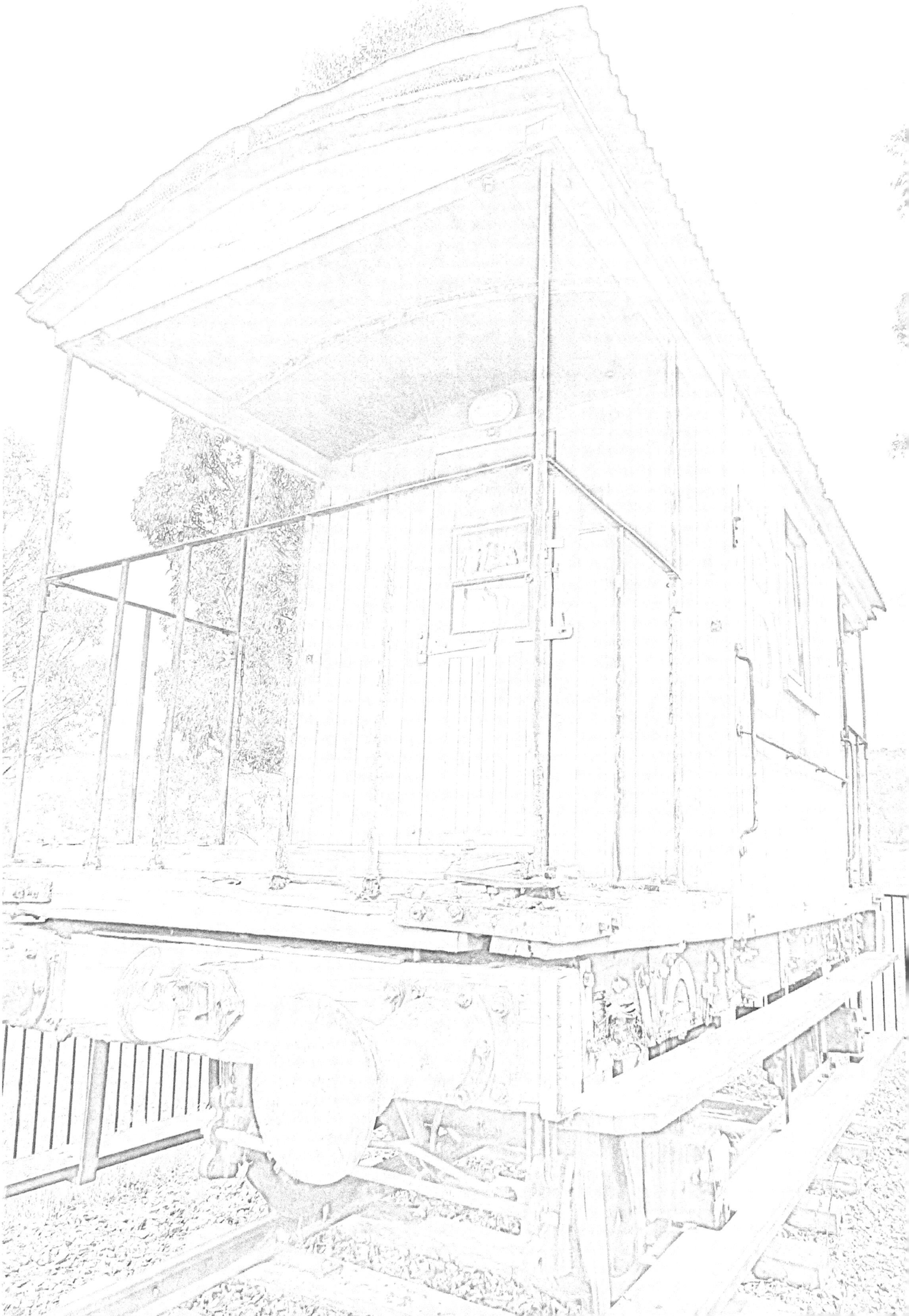

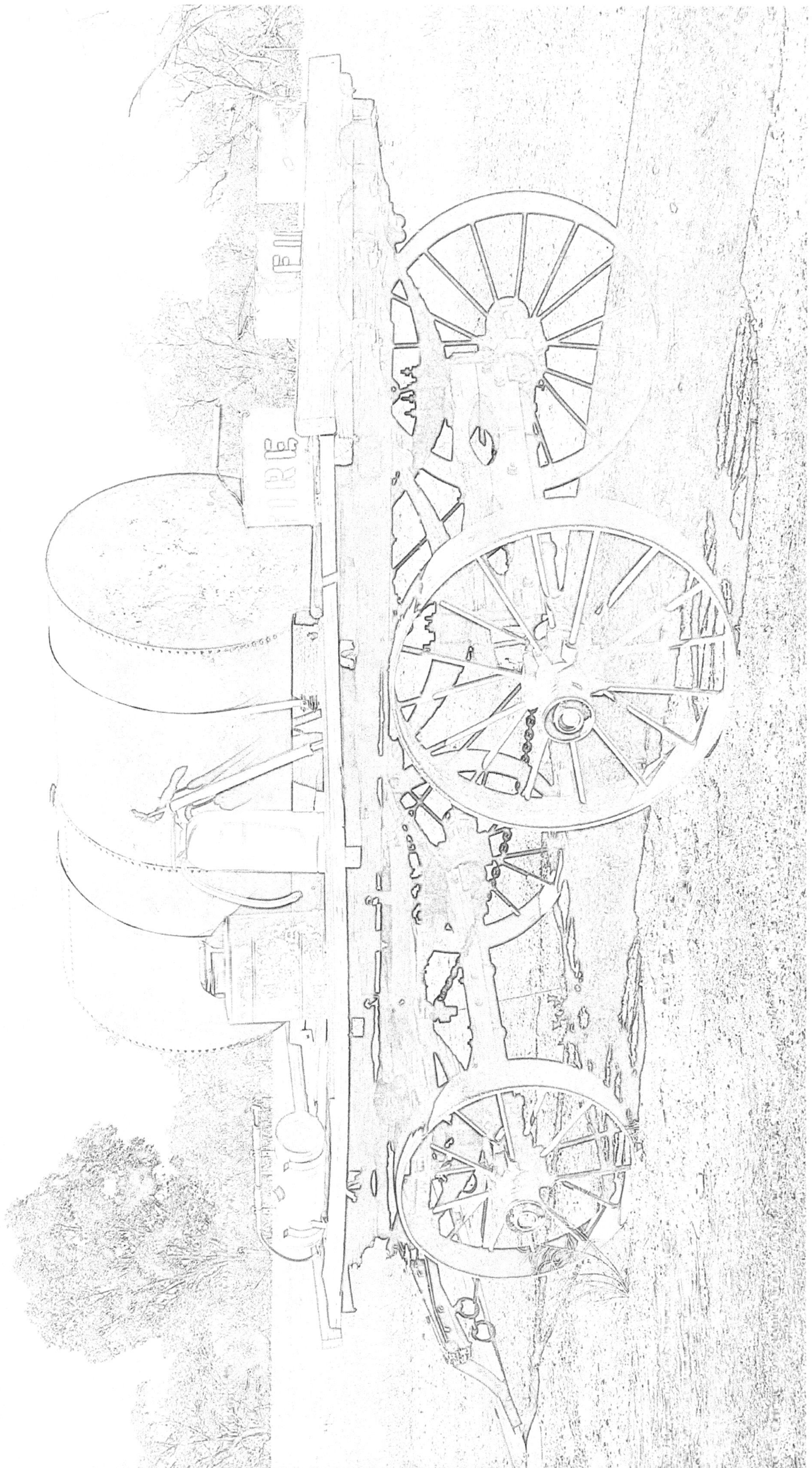

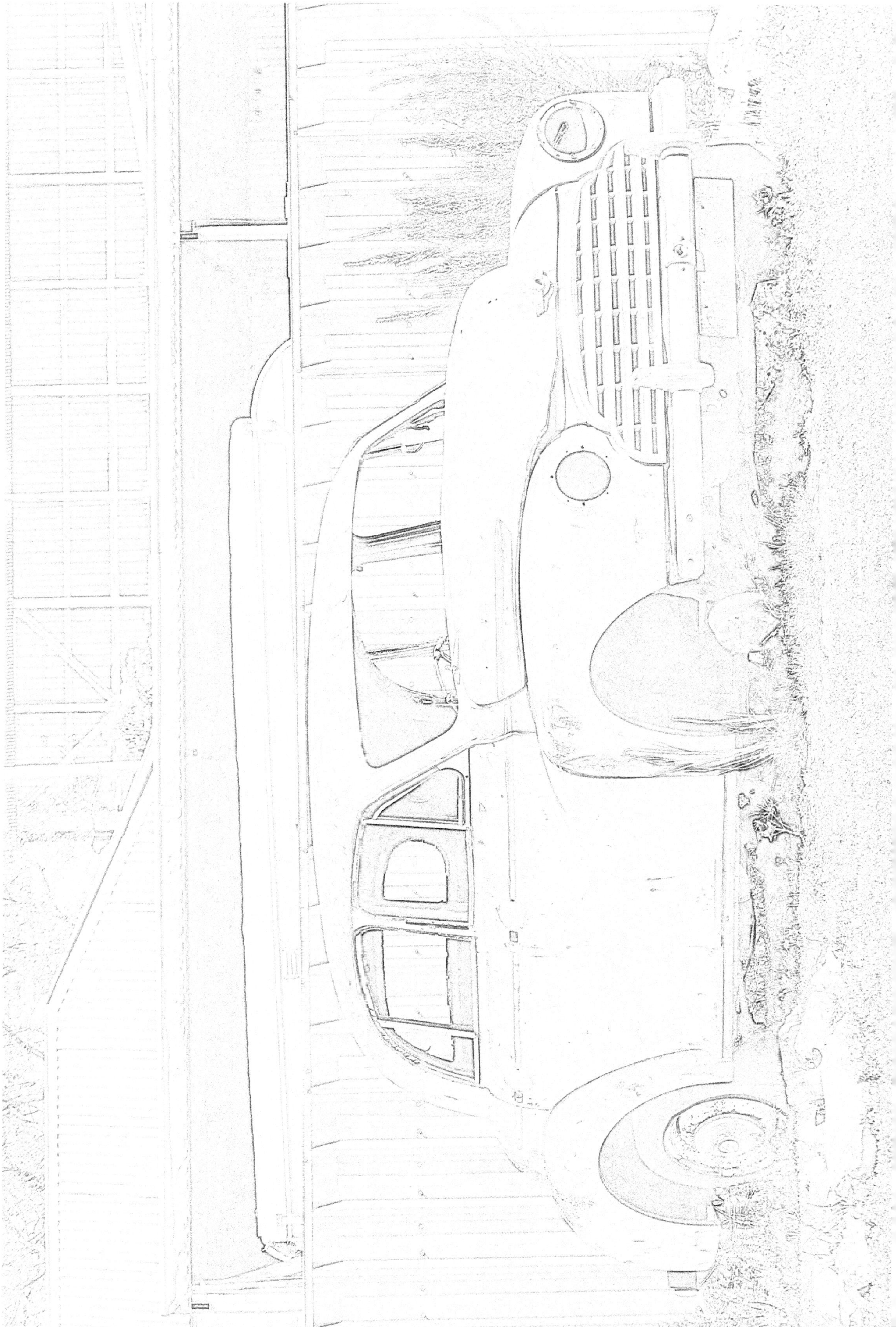

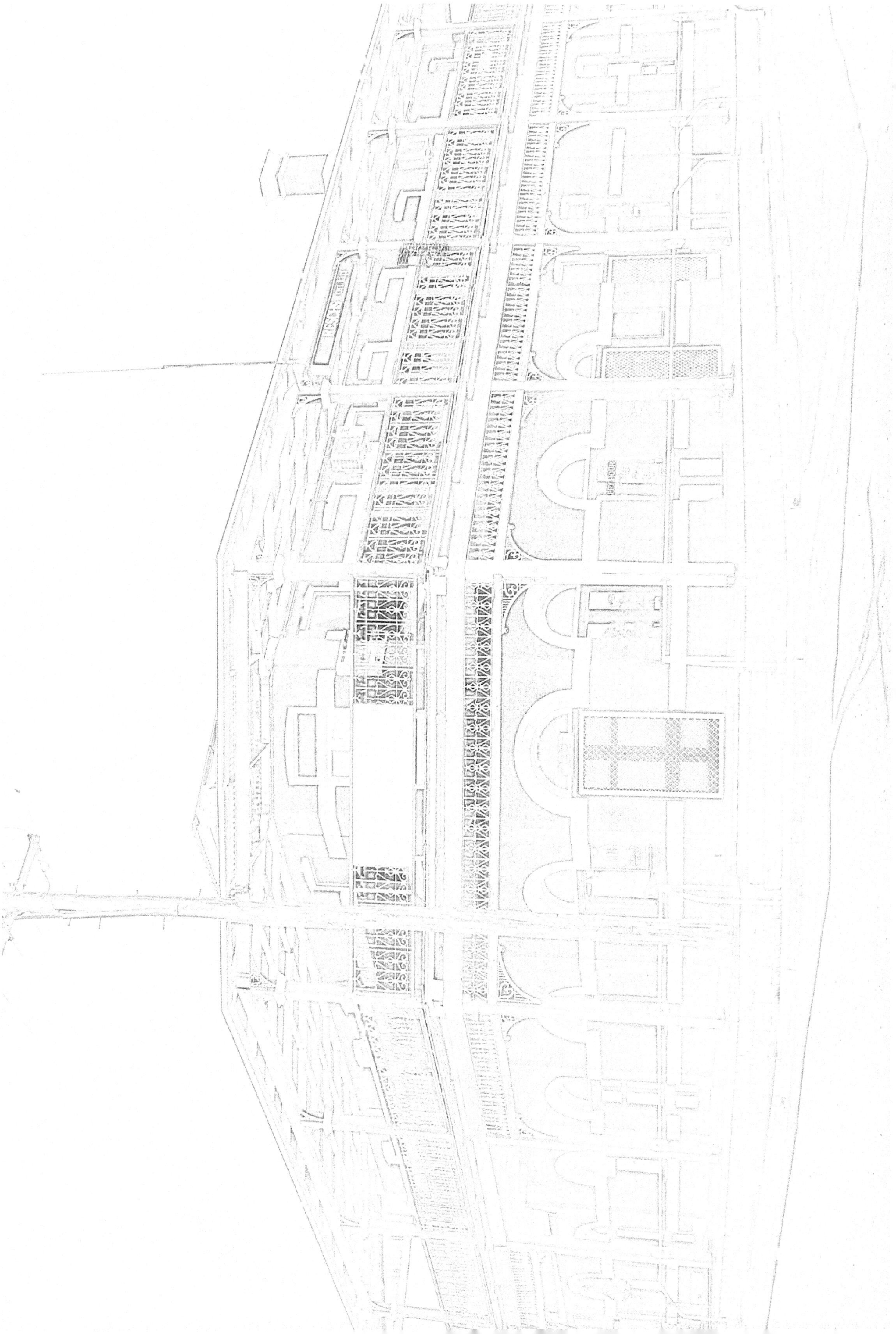

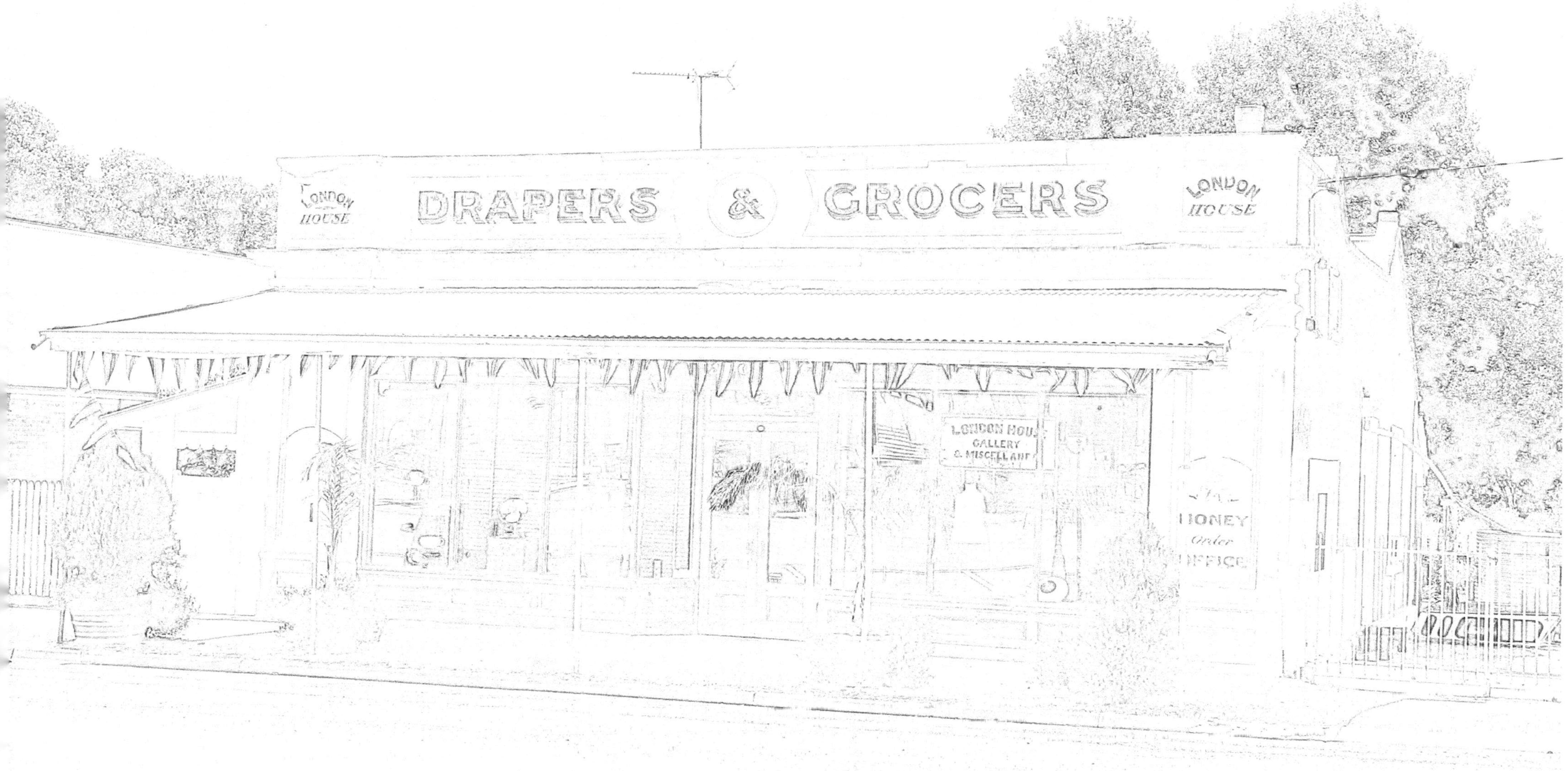
LONDON HOUSE
DRAPERS & GROCERS
LONDON HOUSE
GALLERY

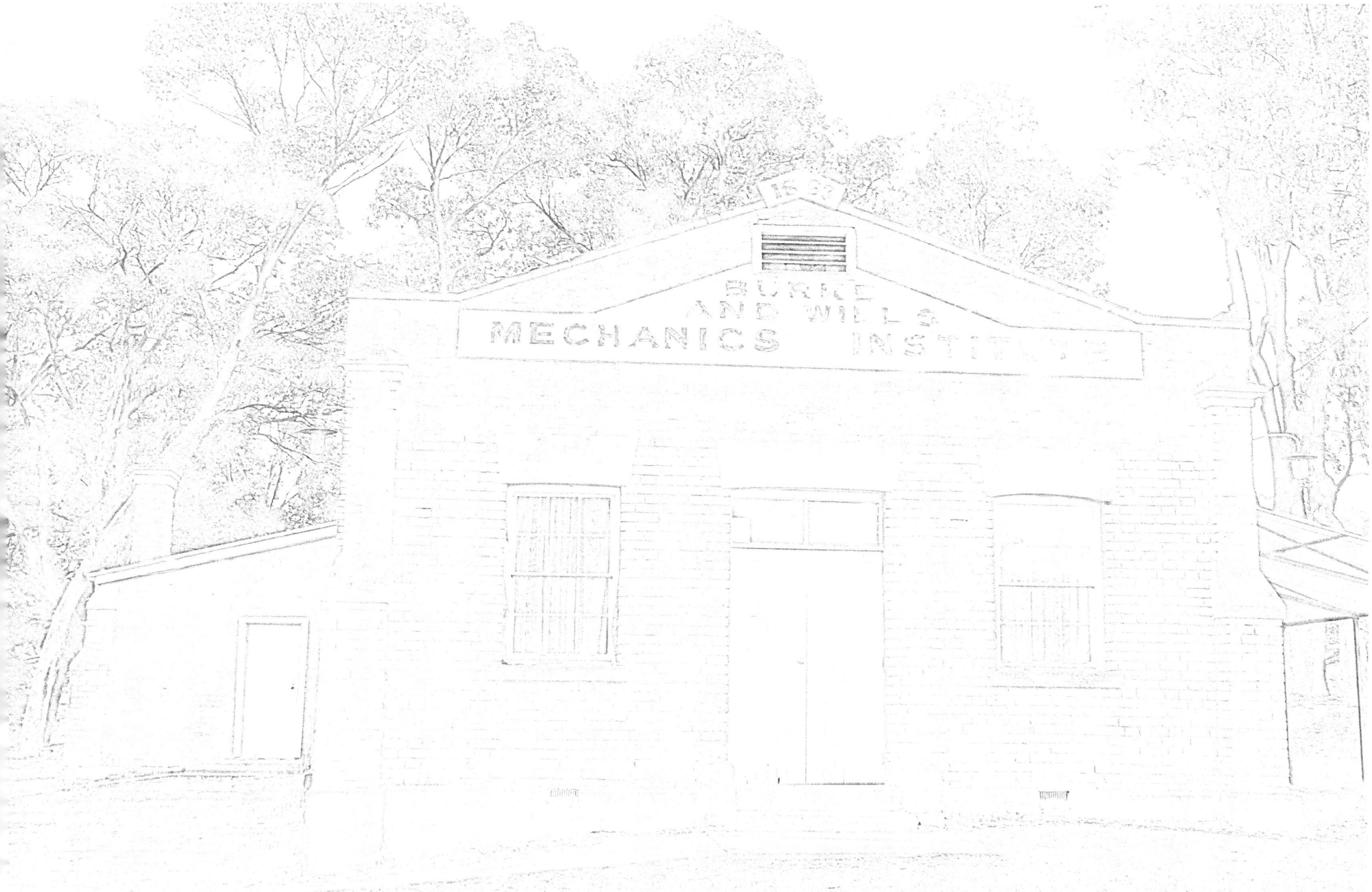
BURKE
AND WILLS
MECHANICS

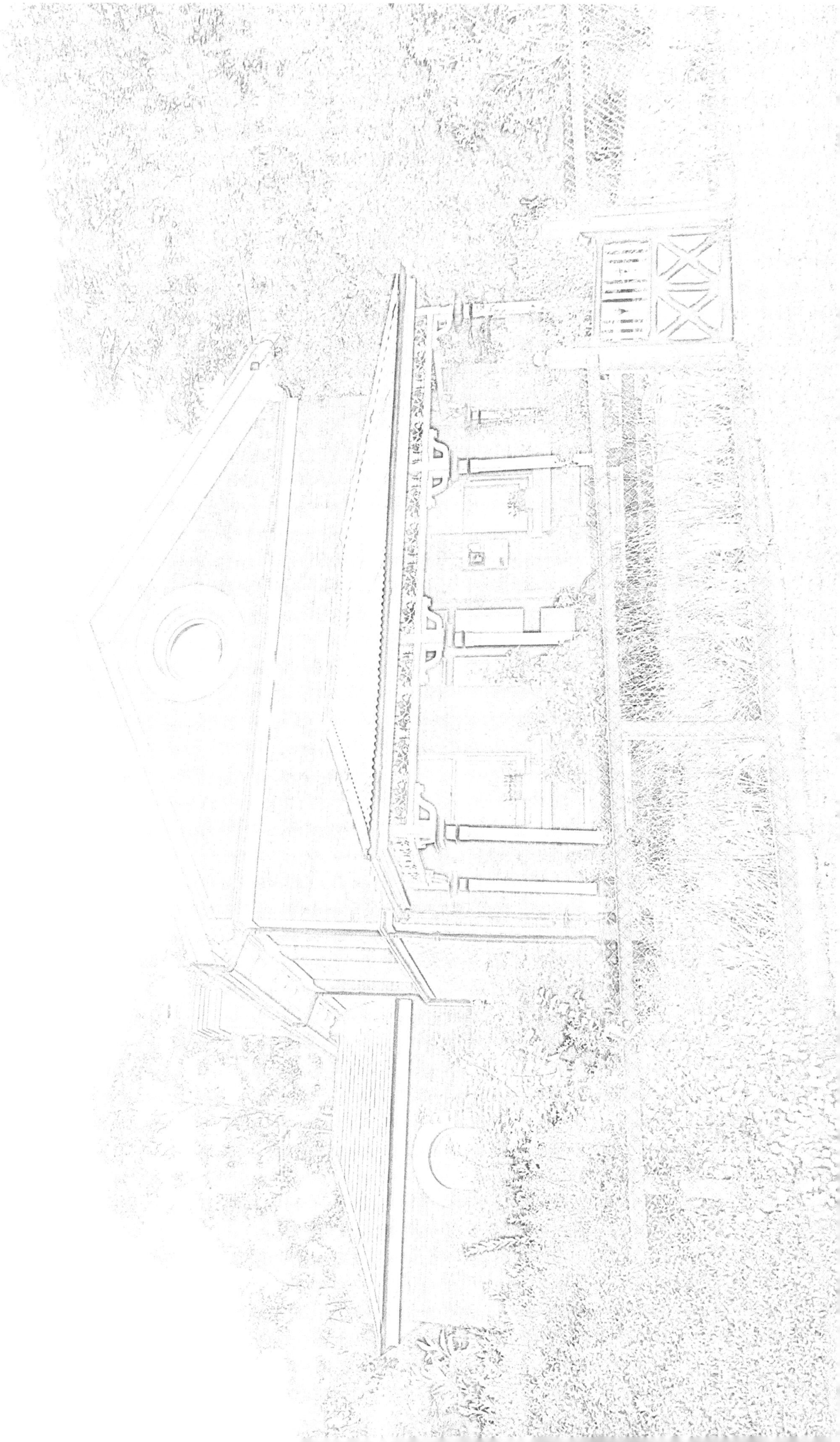

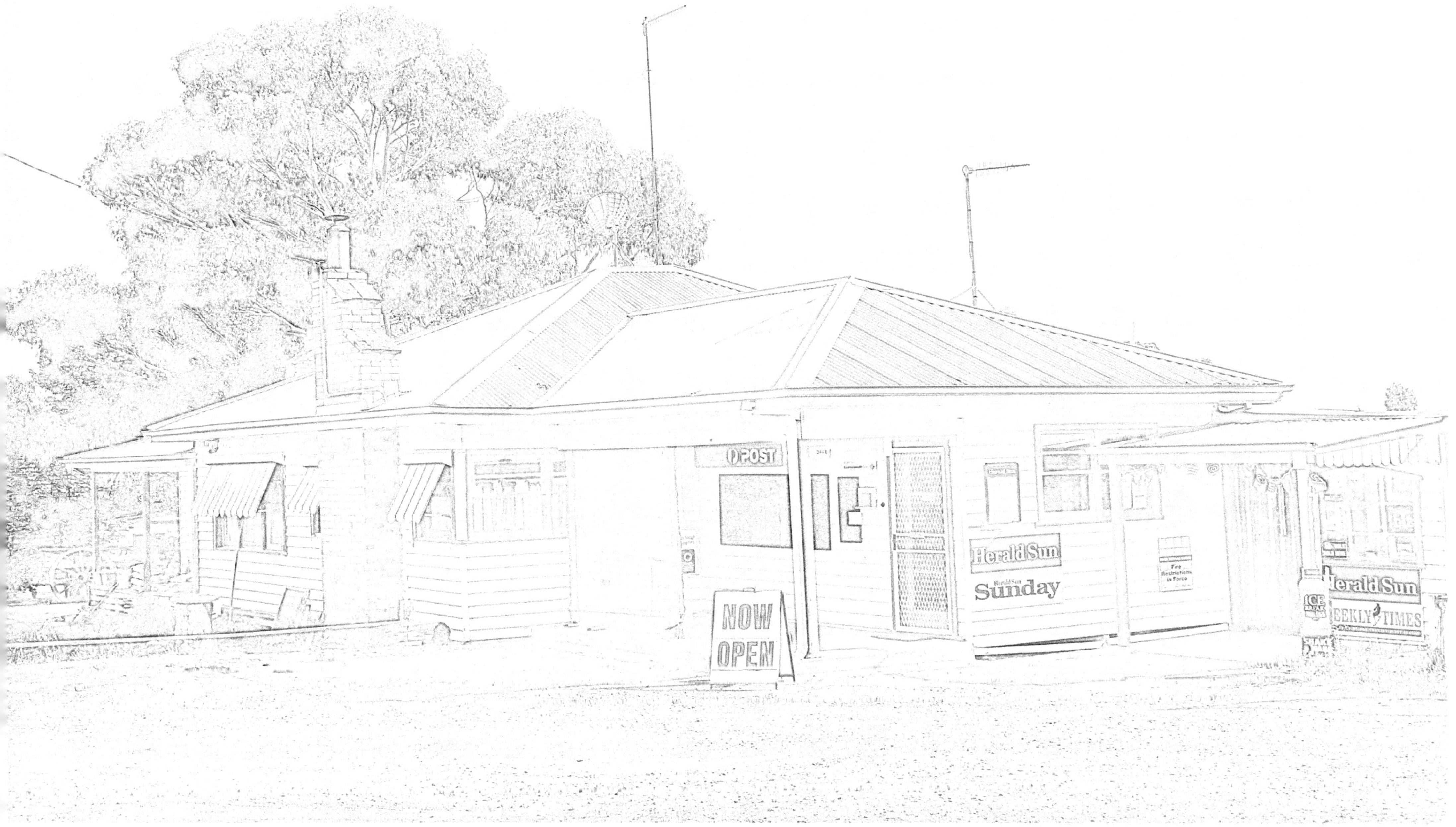
POST
NOW OPEN
Herald Sun
Herald Sun Sunday
Fire Restrictions in Force
ICE
Herald Sun
EEKLY TIMES

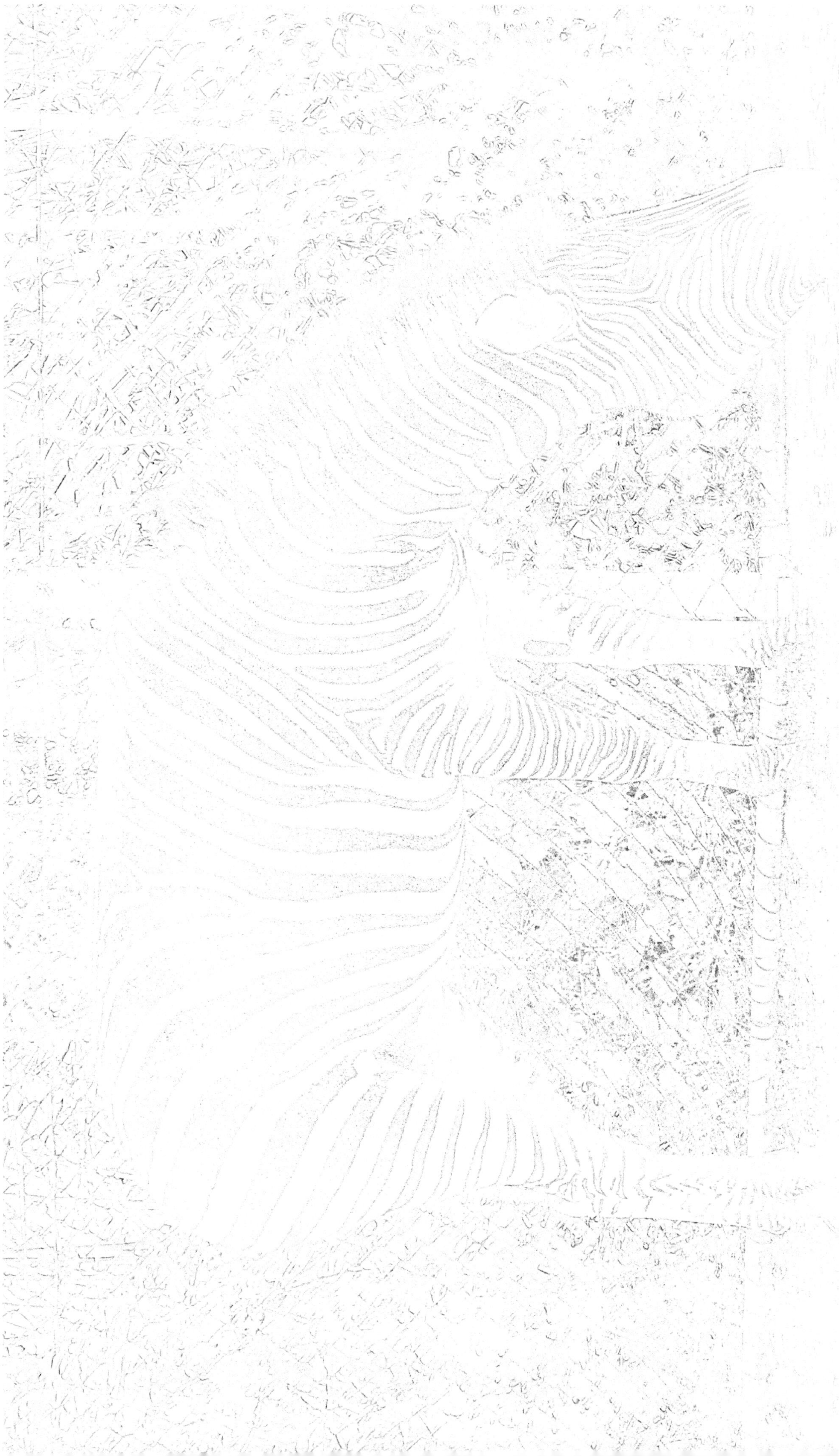

VB
BOTTLE SHOP

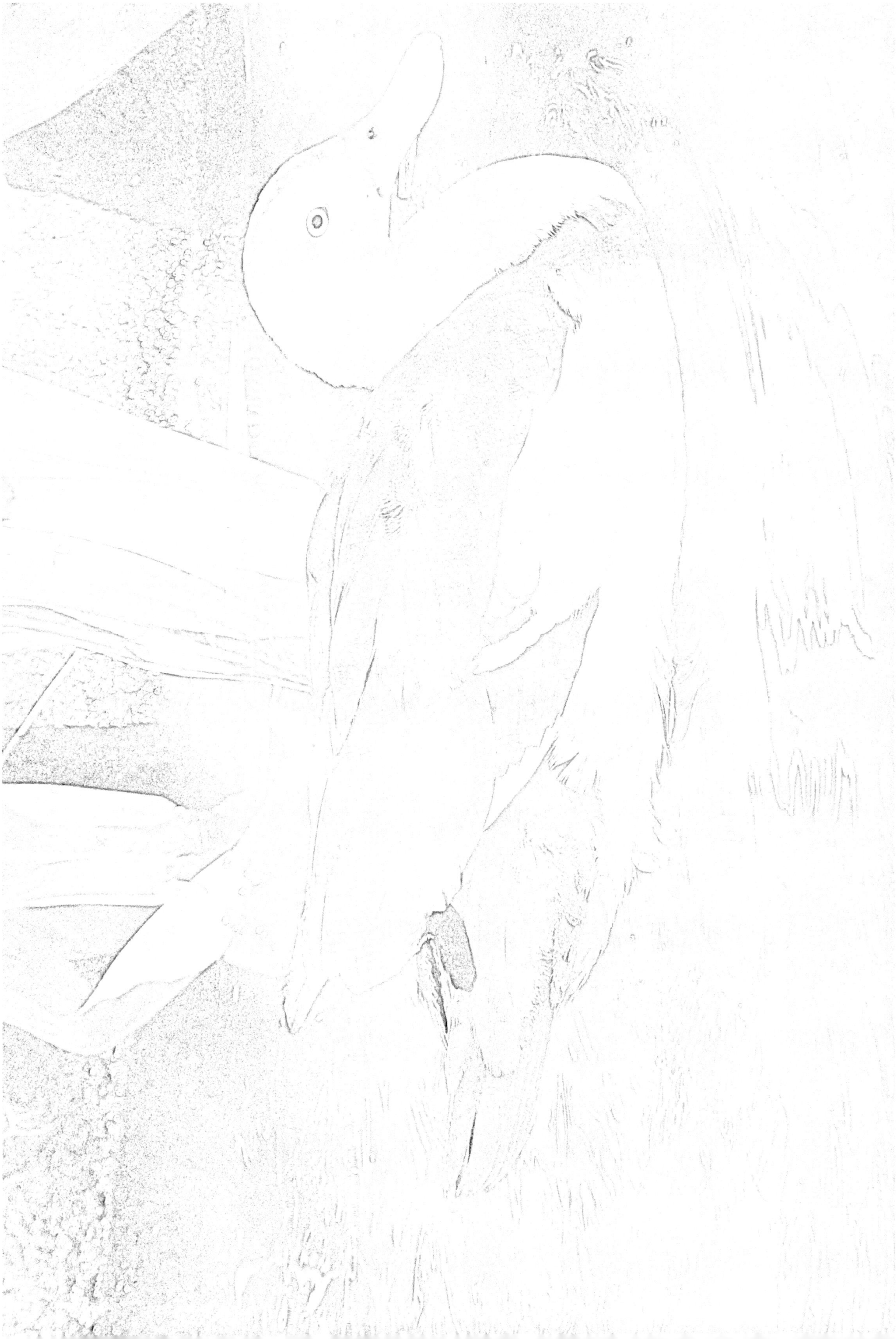

www.ingramcontent.com/pod-product-compliance
Lightning Source LLC
Chambersburg PA
CBHW081051180526
45170CB00005B/1759
* 9 7 8 0 3 5 9 8 2 3 6 7 3 *